The Improv Series
MODAL SOLOING STRATEGIES F

Modern Ideas for All Styles
JODY FISHER

Alfred, the leader in educational publishing, and the National Guitar Workshop, one of America's finest guitar schools, have joined forces to bring you the best, most progressive educational tools possible. We hope you will enjoy this book and encourage you to look for other fine products from Alfred and the National Guitar Workshop.

This book was acquired, edited, and produced by Workshop Arts, Inc., the publishing arm of the National Guitar Workshop.

Nathaniel Gunod, acquisitions, managing editor

Burgess Speed, acquisitions, senior editor

Timothy Phelps, interior design

Ante Gelo, music typesetter

CD tracks 1, 4, 7, 10, 13, 16, 19, and 22 recorded by Robert Brown at Workshop Sounds Studio, Cranford, NJ; tracks 2, 3, 5, 6, 11, 12, 14, 15, 17, and 18 recorded at Studio Blue, Derry Hill, TX; tracks 8 and 9 recorded by Glenn Riley; tracks 20 and 21 recorded by Steve Robertson at Standing Room Only Studios, Fontana, CA

Alfred Music Publishing Co., Inc.
P.O. Box 10003
Van Nuys, CA 91410-0003
alfred.com

ISBN-10: 0-7390-7162-9 (Book & CD)
ISBN-13: 978-0-7390-7162-5 (Book & CD)

CONTENTS

ABOUT THE AUTHOR

Jody Fisher has worked professionally in virtually all styles of music during his career, from straight-ahead and contemporary jazz to rock 'n' roll, country, and pop. For several years, he was a director of the National Guitar Workshop. He also taught guitar and jazz studies at both the University of Redlands and Idyllwild School of Music and the Arts (ISOMATA). He is an active performer in the Southern California area, where he maintains a busy private teaching practice as well.

PHOTO BY LARRY LYTLE

Acknowledgements

One does not survive in the music business without help and support from a large network of family and friends. I would like to thank my wife, Julie; my son, Josh; Shauna Perry; and my parents, Howard and Edith Fisher. Also, thanks to my brother, Rich; my uncle, Sid; David Smolover, Nat Gunod, Ted Greene, Joe Diorio, George Stanley, Bob Scarano; and the entire gang at Caleb's Guitar.

Other Instructional Materials by Jody Fisher

30-Day Guitar Workout (Alfred/National Guitar Workshop—Book #17867)

Ear Training for the Contemporary Guitarist (Alfred/National Guitar Workshop—Book & CD #19370)

Jazz Skills (National Guitar Workshop—Book & CD #07-1012)

Rhythm Guitar Encyclopedia (Alfred/National Guitar Workshop—Book & 2 CDs #14838)

Stand Alone Tracks: Smooth Jazz (Alfred/National Guitar Workshop—Book & CD #17808)

The Complete Jazz Method:

    Beginning Jazz Guitar (Alfred/National Guitar Workshop—Book & CD #14120)

    Intermediate Jazz Guitar (Alfred/National Guitar Workshop—Book & CD #14123)

    Mastering Jazz Guitar: Chord/Melody (Alfred/National Guitar Workshop—Book & CD #14126)

    Mastering Jazz Guitar: Improvisation (Alfred/National Guitar Workshop—Book & CD #14129)

Jazz Guitar Harmony (Alfred/National Guitar Workshop—Book & CD #20440)

Teaching Guitar (Alfred/National Guitar Workshop—Book & CD #22916)

Jazz Licks Encyclopedia (Alfred/National Guitar Workshop—Book & CD #19420)

A compact disc is included with this book. Use the CD to help ensure you're capturing the feel of the examples and interpreting the rhythms correctly. The symbol shown at the left appears next to every example that is on the CD. The track number below the symbol corresponds directly to the example you want to hear. Track 1 provides tuning notes for your guitar.

INTRODUCTION

Welcome to *Modal Soloing Strategies for Guitar*, the only book about the modes you may ever need. This book is for intermediate to advanced guitarists desiring a thorough understanding of modes and their applications for improvising. For those unfamiliar with the basics of notation and music theory, there is a review starting on the next page. If you are already familiar with these basics, you can skip the review and jump ahead to page 20.

The modes have been in existence for centuries as compositional tools for classical, folk, and ethnic musicians, as improvisational devices for jazz musicians, and a source of "new" sounds for rock, pop, and country artists. But, unfortunately, the subject has been shrouded in mystery, causing many guitar students a lot of confusion. The confusion may be due to an incomplete overview of the subject. There are many ways of looking at modes and each one has an important place in understanding and applying the modes to improvising, composition, or both. Although modes can be derived from both major and minor scales, this book deals only with the modes of the major scale. Each chapter is devoted to a particular mode and will include:

- A notated list of the mode in twelve keys
- Perspective #1: The modal formula, a look at where the half steps occur in the scale and how it relates horizontally to the fretboard
- Perspective #2: The mode's relationship to the diatonic harmony
- Perspective #3: The mode created by altering another scale
- Perspective #4: The mode's intervallic distance from the "parent" key, measuring from the root of a chord
- Perspective #5: Deducing a mode's key signature
- Six closed-position fingerings
- Open-position fingerings in every key
- The harmonized mode, with sample chord voicings
- Mode usage
- Practice suggestions
- Licks
- Melodic patterns
- Backing track to practice soloing

Also, sample solos utilizing most of the modes in various combinations have been included at the end of the book.

One way this book is different from many others is that three fingering options are covered. The first is the horizontal approach along the single string. The second is the use of "locked" fingerings or scales that are played in a fixed position. The third fingering option is the "open" position. When any musical concept is explored on the guitar, a more complete understanding is accomplished by examining all three fingering options.

It should be noted here that, while a clear understanding of the modes is important, it represents only a part of what is needed to become an accomplished improviser. Modes, in conjunction with other scales, arpeggios, and licks, are only part of the picture. Improvisation is a lifetime study. Try to keep this in mind.

Each chapter of this book is complete so it's all right to skip around. You can also move straight through from beginning to end for a very comprehensive study. To get the most out of this book, you need to transpose all exercises and fingerings in all twelve keys. At first this may seem like a hassle, but in time it will get easier and pay off in the form of greater fluency.

NOTATION AND THEORY REVIEW

Tablature (TAB)

Tablature (TAB) is a system of notation that graphically represents the strings and frets of the guitar fingerboard. Each note is indicated by placing a number, which indicates the fret to play, on the appropriate string.

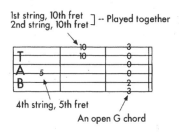

Scale Diagrams

This book is loaded with scale diagrams. The top line represents the first string of the guitar, and the bottom line the sixth. The vertical lines represent frets, which are numbered with Roman numerals.

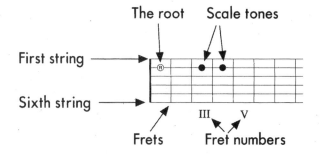

Chord Diagrams

Chord diagrams are similar to scale diagrams, except they are oriented vertically instead of horizontally. Vertical lines represent strings, and horizontal lines represent frets. Roman numerals are used to number the frets.

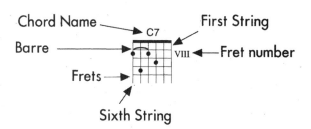

Reading Roman Numerals

Here is a review of Roman numerals and their Arabic equivalents.

Roman Numeral Review		
I or i................ 1		V or v............ 5
II or ii............ 2		VI or vi.......... 6
III or iii........... 3		VII or vii........ 7
IV or iv........... 4		

Left-Hand Techniques

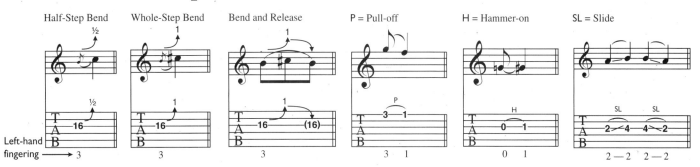

The Chromatic Scale

In our western music system, we have twelve tones that are repeated over and over spanning many octaves. We call this set of tones the *chromatic scale.* All of the notes in the chromatic scale are one half step (one fret on the guitar) away from each other. Obviously, two half steps would equal a whole step.

Below is a chromatic scale covering one octave (starting and ending on the same tone). Two note names (A♯/B♭, C♯/D♭, etc.) indicate *enharmonic tones,* or two different notes with the same exact pitch. In other words, these notes sound the same but are spelled differently.

Example 1

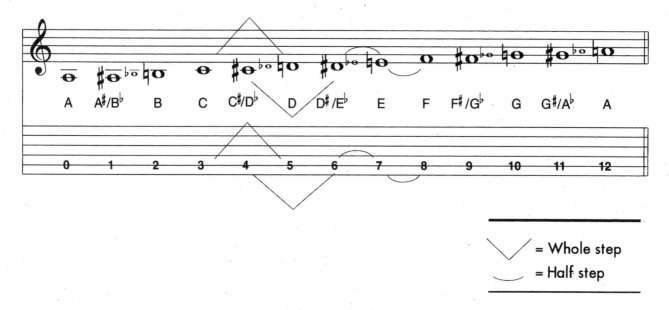

The Major Scale

Most of our musical resources are derived from the *major scale.* A major scale can begin on any one of the twelve tones found in the chromatic scale. The whole step/half step formula for a major scale is (1 = whole, 1/2 = half):

$$1 \quad 1 \quad 1/2 \quad 1 \quad 1 \quad 1 \quad 1/2$$

In Example 2 (next page), we are building a C Major scale. We start with the note C. Then we move one whole step up to find the next note, which is D. Another whole step will bring us to the note E. One half step away from E is F. (Take a look at Example 1 and you will notice there are no sharp or flat notes between E and F, and B and C). Continuing, a whole step up from F is G, and then another whole step up bring us to A, and yet another brings us to B. Our last move will be a half step up from B to C. We have just constructed a C Major scale.

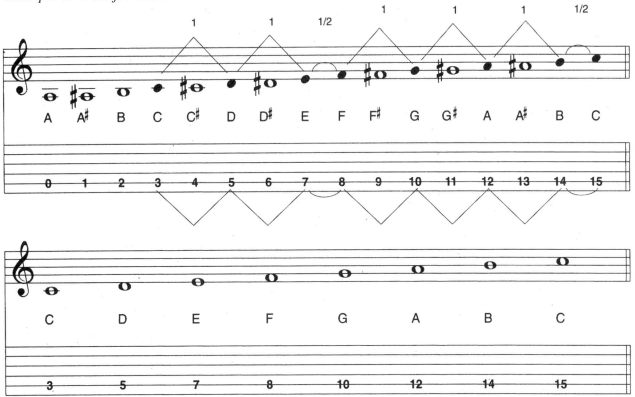

Using the same process as above, we can create a major scale by starting on any note of the chromatic scale. For instance, if we start on E♭ instead of C, we get an E♭ Major scale.

Example 3: E♭ Major Scale

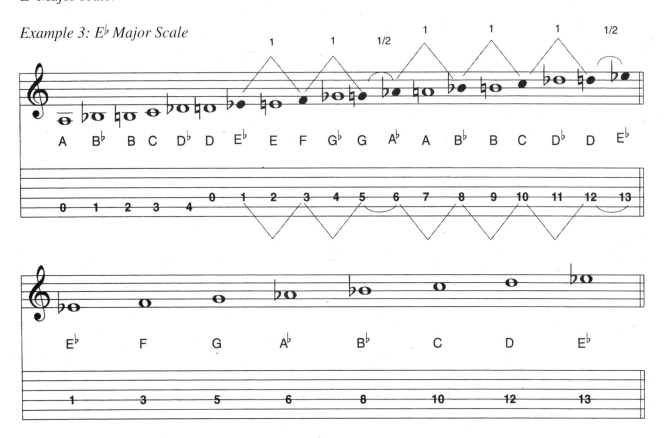

What you need to do now is construct all twelve major scales on paper, away from your guitar. Construct them in the following order: C, F, B♭, E♭, A♭, D♭, G♭, B, E, A, D and G*. Check your results against the example below, and start memorizing them by recitation away from your instrument. This cannot be over stressed. Almost all theoretical concepts—and that certainly includes the modes—will be based on this information, and the better you know these scales, the easier your musical studies will be.

Here are the major scales. The music and TAB can be found in Example 4 on page 9 . Memorize, memorize, memorize.

C Major	C D E F G A B C
F Major	F G A B♭ C D E F
B♭ Major	B♭ C D E♭ F G A B♭
E♭ Major	E♭ F G A♭ B♭ C D E♭
A♭ Major	A♭ B♭ C D♭ E♭ F G A♭
D♭ Major	D♭ E♭ F G♭ A♭ B♭ C D♭
G♭ Major	G♭ A♭ B♭ C♭ D♭ E♭ F G♭
B Major	B C♯ D♯ E F♯ G♯ A♯ B
E Major	E F♯ G♯ A B C♯ D♯ E
A Major	A B C♯ D E F♯ G♯ A
D Major	D E F♯ G A B C♯ D
G Major	G A B C D E F♯ G

* Note: When arranged in the order above, the number of flats in each flat scale increases by one, and the number of sharps in each sharp scale decreases by one. This is a helpful memory tool. Notice that each scale starts four steps above the last (from C to F is four steps: C, D, E, F). This is called a "cycle of fourths," and many of the concepts in this book are presented in this order.

Example 4

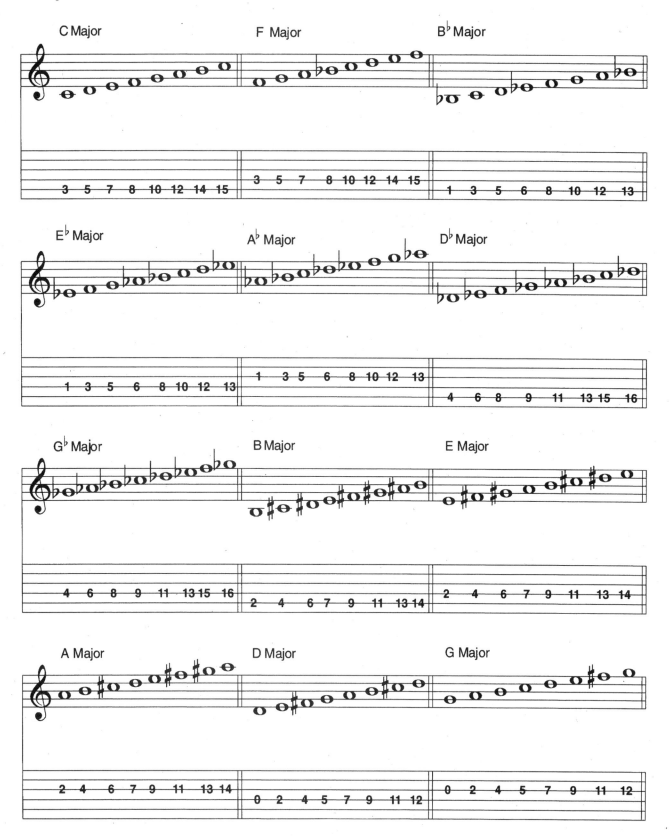

Key Signatures

The area between the clef and the time signature at the beginning of a piece of music is called the *key signature*. The sharps or flats found in the key signature are derived from the major scale that is the basis for the song. The number of sharps or flats will tell you the key of the song. Each key designation corresponds to one of the major scales. In other words, if you see three sharps in the key signature, you know the song is in the key of A, because the A Major scale has three sharps. Four flats means the song is in A♭. The absence of sharps or flats means the song is in the key of C, because there are no sharps or flats in the C Major scale.

Later in this chapter, we will deal with minor scales. Every key signature is shared by one major key (scale) and one minor key (scale). As you will see in this book, we can also relate modes to key signatures, but for now we will concern ourselves only with the minor keys that relate to the major key signatures.

For every major key, there is a relative minor key that is built on the sixth tone of the major scale for the key. For instance, in the key of C, the note A is the sixth tone (C D E F G A), so A Minor is the relative minor key of C Major. The example below shows all the key signatures with their corresponding major and minor keys.

Key Signature	Major Key	Minor Key	Key Signature	Major Key	Minor Key
(no sharps/flats)	C	A	(1 flat)	F	D
(1 sharp)	G	E	(2 flats)	B♭	G
(2 sharps)	D	B	(3 flats)	E♭	C
(3 sharps)	A	F♯	(4 flats)	A♭	F
(4 sharps)	E	C♯	(5 flats)	D♭	B♭
(5 sharps)	B	G♯	(6 flats)	G♭	E♭

Intervals

An *interval* is the distance between two notes. An interval name describes the distance. It is important to be able to recognize intervals by both sight and sound, and to know where they lie on the fingerboard. When determining an interval's name, be sure to include both notes in the count, starting with the bottom note and counting upward. The following is a list of intervals. On page 12, you will find guitar neck diagrams showing these intervals on the guitar.

Example 5

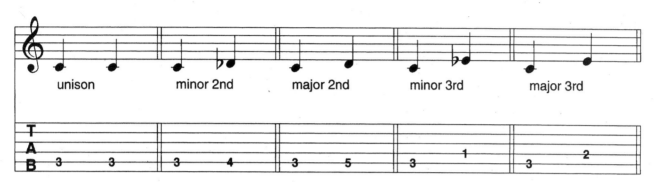

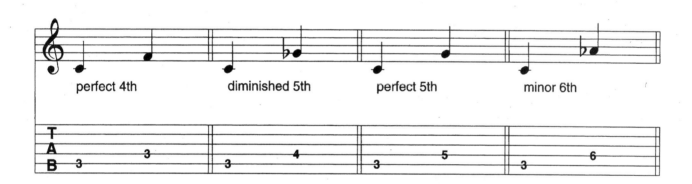

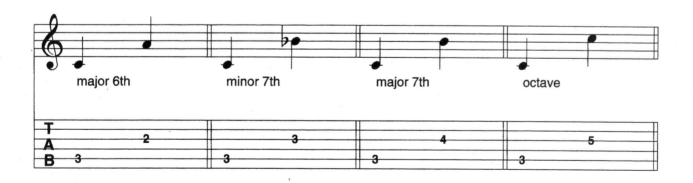

As in Example 5, the following intervals are all built up from the note C. Here, however, each interval is shown in two different octaves. As you will see, this is done to show the different fingerings that result from the tuning of the guitar. There is a major third between the third and second string, but all the other strings are a perfect fourth apart. Because of this, you will have to learn special fingerings for some of the intervals that involve the third and/or second string.

Example 6

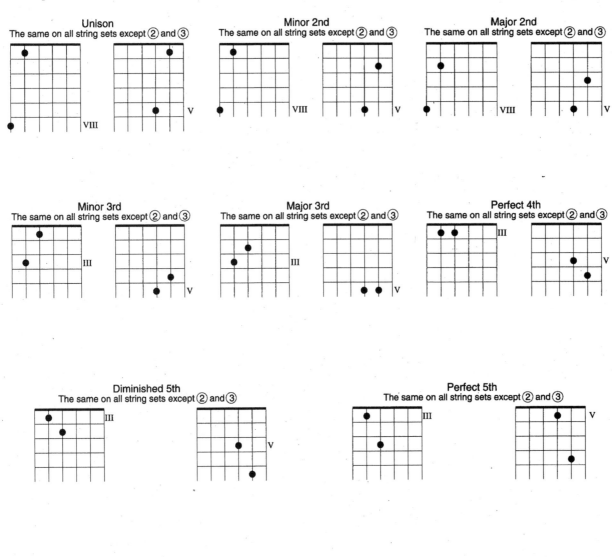

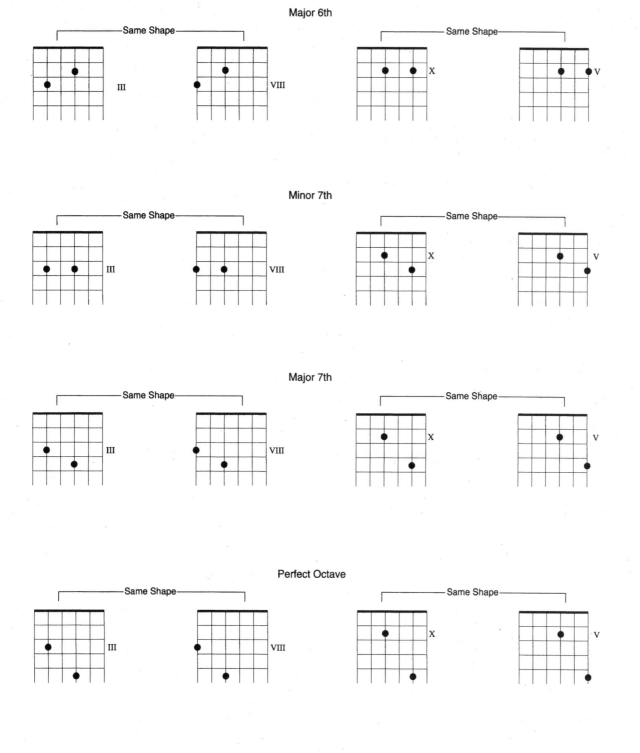

Inversions

To create a different sound using the same notes, you can *invert* (turn upside down) an interval, thereby changing its quality. If you find this section difficult to follow, come back to it after you are very familiar with the major scale in all the keys. (To be able to measure intervals easily, you need a thorough understanding of the major scale, since we use it for the bottom note of an interval as a measuring device.)

An *inversion* of an interval is created by raising the lower note one octave or by lowering the top note one octave.

Example 7

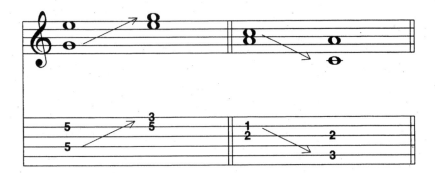

In Example 7, the distance between G and E in the G Major scale is that of a major sixth. Inverting this interval and then using the E Major scale to measure the new interval, we find the interval is now a minor third. In the second example, using the A Major scale, we find the distance between A and C to be a minor third. After inversion, using the C Major scale to measure up from the bottom note will reveal the new interval to be a major sixth.

An easy way to figure our interval inversions is to realize that the sum of both intervals—the original interval and the inverted interval—will always equal nine. An inverted second will become a seventh (2 + 7 = 9), and an inverted third will become a sixth (3 + 6 = 9), etc.

1	2	3	4	5	6	7	8
+ 8	7	6	5	4	3	2	1
9	9	9	9	9	9	9	9

Also, the quality (whether it is major, minor, or perfect) will change to its opposite, except for perfect intervals; they will remain perfect. In other words:

> Major becomes Minor
> Minor becomes Major
> Perfect remains Perfect

Example 8

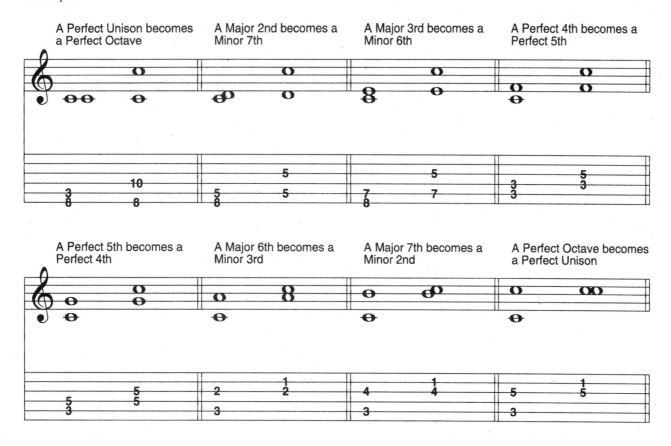

A Perfect Unison becomes a Perfect Octave

A Major 2nd becomes a Minor 7th

A Major 3rd becomes a Minor 6th

A Perfect 4th becomes a Perfect 5th

A Perfect 5th becomes a Perfect 4th

A Major 6th becomes a Minor 3rd

A Major 7th becomes a Minor 2nd

A Perfect Octave becomes a Perfect Unison

Diminished Intervals

Another type, or quality, of interval is the *diminished* interval. If a minor or perfect interval is made one half step smaller, we refer to it as being a diminished interval.

Example 9

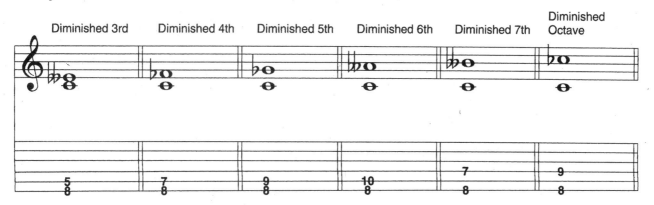

Diminished 3rd   Diminished 4th   Diminished 5th   Diminished 6th   Diminished 7th   Diminished Octave

Augmented Intervals

There is one more interval quality to look at: the *augmented* interval. If a major or perfect interval is raised one half step, we refer to it as being augmented.

Example 10

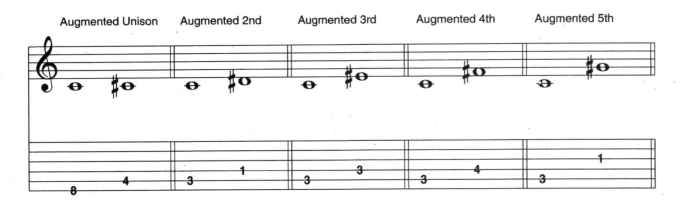

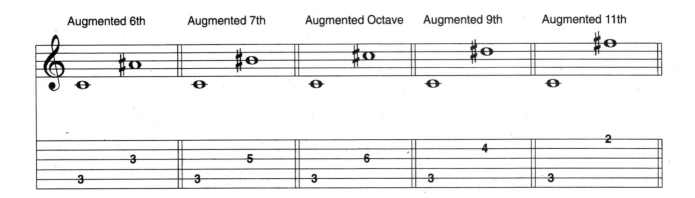

Inversions of Diminished and Augmented Intervals

As with other intervals, diminished and augmented intervals may be inverted. Once again, the sum of both numbers will always be nine, and the quality will change to its opposite.

Example 11

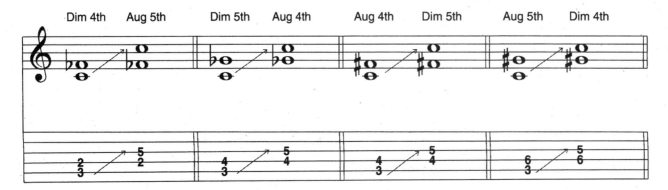

Minor Scales

Although we will only be covering the modes of the major scale in this book, it is also beneficial to have a solid foundation in the minor scales, as many concepts relating to the minor scales can also relate to the modes.

The Natural Minor Scale

To find a natural minor scale, simply start on the sixth degree of any major scale and proceed to the same note one octave higher. Another way is to follow this formula of whole steps and half steps:

$$1 \quad 1/2 \quad 1 \quad 1 \quad 1/2 \quad 1 \quad 1$$

This is exactly the same as the Aeolian Mode, but don't worry about this for now. For every major key, there is a corresponding minor key that shares the same key signature. This is known as the *relative major/minor relationship.* The major scale corresponds to the major key, and the natural minor scale corresponds to the minor key. A song with no sharps or flats in the key signature is either in the key of C Major or A Minor. You use your ear to determine the major or minor tonality.

Example 12

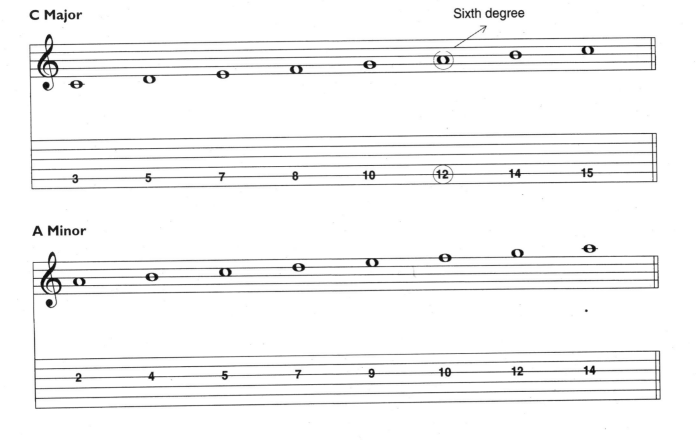

An F Major scale would produce a D Natural Minor Scale, a B♭ Major scale would produce a G Natural Minor scale, etc. It would be a good idea to memorize all of the relative major and minor scales. This will make your future studies much easier.

The Harmonic Minor Scale

The easiest way to conceive the *harmonic minor scale* is to start with a natural minor scale and raise the seventh degree. You could also use the formula:

1 1/2 1 1 1/2 1+1/2 1/2

↑

The distance of one and a
half steps, or a minor 3rd

Example 13

Natural Minor

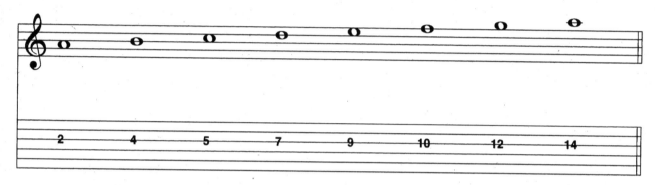

Harmonic Minor

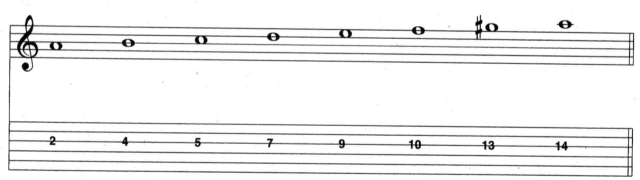

The harmonic minor scale has a *leading tone* (the ♮7), which has a stronger pull to the root than the ♭7, giving this type of minor scale a stronger sense of key.

The Melodic Minor and "Jazz Minor" Scales

The melodic minor scale is most easily constructed by starting with a natural minor scale and raising the sixth and seventh degrees, but only in ascending form. The descending form returns to the natural minor. The reasons for this have to do with compositional devices and are beyond the scope of this book. The formula for the ascending form of this scale is.

1 1/2 1 1 1 1 1/2

Example 14

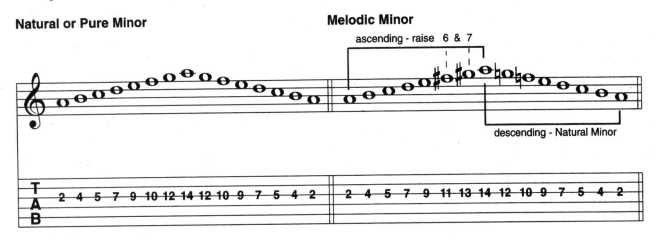

The "jazz minor" scale is the same as the ascending melodic minor scale. The only difference is that the raised degrees remain raised in the descending form. Most musicians do not use the term "jazz minor." In this book, understand the term "melodic minor" refers to the "jazz minor" form.

Example 15

THE IONIAN MODE

In Every Key on Single Strings

When thinking in a modal context, the major scale is thought of as the Ionian mode.
Here is the mode in all the keys. The keys are arranged in a cycle of fourths.

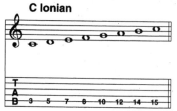

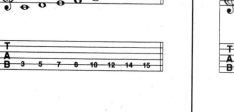

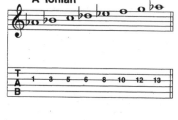

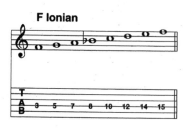

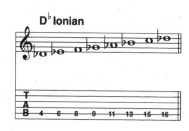

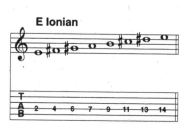

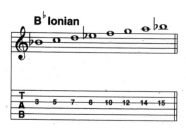

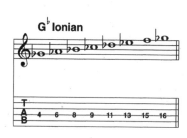

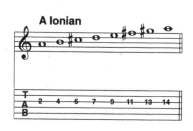

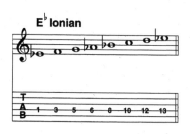

G♭ and F♯ are enharmonically equivalent. The notes sound the same but are named differently.

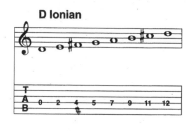

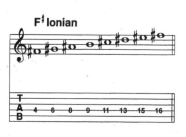

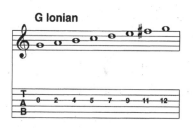

Note: For each mode, there are five "perspectives." These perspectives provide different ways of looking at the same mode.

Perspective #1: Finding the Half Steps

The formula for the Ionian mode is 1–1–1/2–1–1–1–1/2. The half steps appear between steps three and four and between seven and eight. Here is the G Ionian mode along each string.

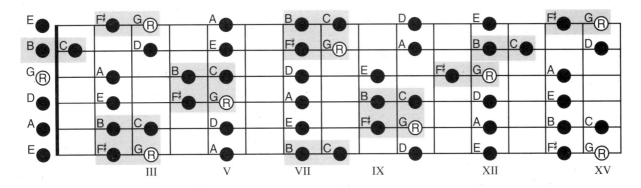

Perspective #2: Thinking in a Parent Key

Major chords function as I or IV chords in major keys. Ionian sounds are found by thinking of a major chord as a I chord. Simply play the major scale that begins on the major chord's root.

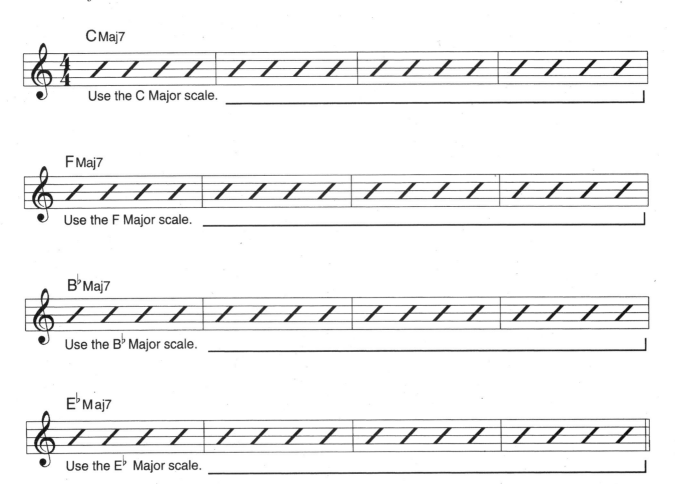

Perspective #3: Altering a Scale

Since the Ionian mode and the major scale are the same, no alteration to the major scale is needed.

Perspective #4: In Relation to a Chord's Root

You can locate the Ionian mode by thinking of the major key signature that has the same name as the chord's root. If you wanted to use B♭ Ionian against a B♭ Maj7 chord, or a B♭ "power chord," think in the key of B♭ Major.

o = root
■ = first note of the
     related major scale

If you were improvising against either of these chords, the Ionian Mode could be thought of as the major scale that begins on this note (B♭).

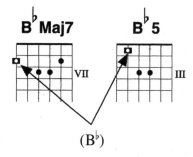

(B♭)

If you were improvising against either of these chords, the Ionian Mode could be thought of as the major scale that begins on this note (C).

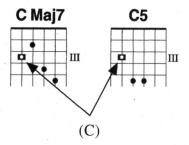

(C)

If you were improvising against either of these chords, the Ionian Mode could be thought of as the major scale that begins on this note (A).

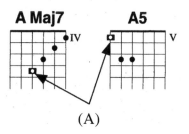

(A)

Perspective #5: Adjusting Key Signatures

There are no adjustments made to a major key signature to find the proper key signature for the Ionian mode since the major scale and the Ionian mode are identical. The key signature for F Ionian is the same as the key signature for F Major. The key signature for A Ionian is the same as the key signature for A Major, etc.

Fingerings: The Mode in Six Closed Positions

Here are six fingerings for the Ionian mode in the key of A. Practice the mode in every key!

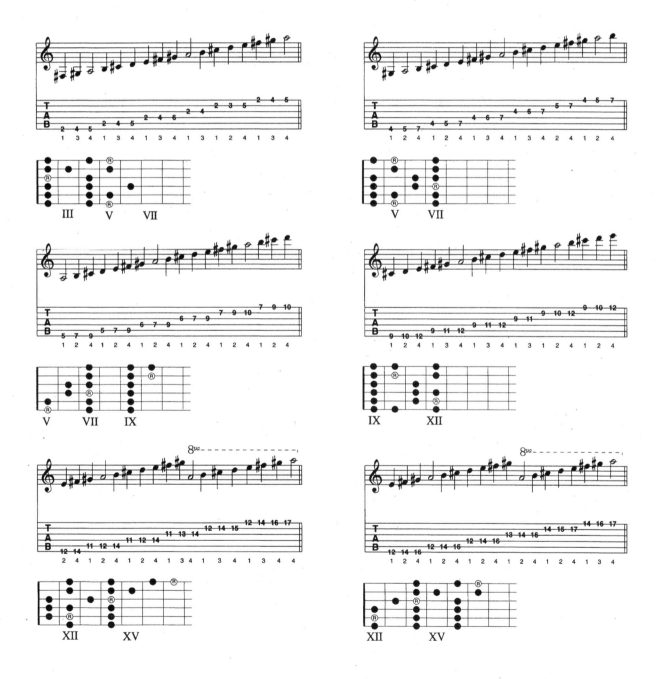

Open Position Fingerings: In Every Key

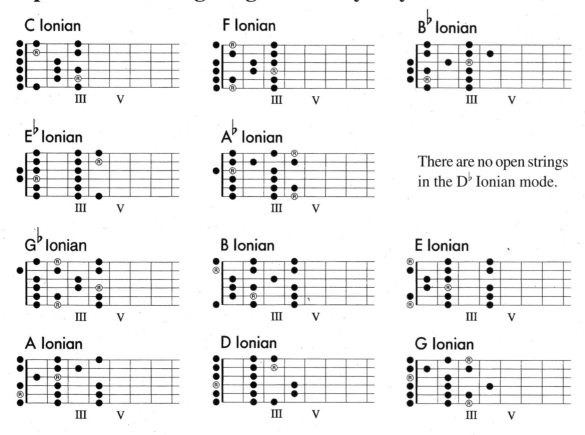

There are no open strings in the D♭ Ionian mode.

Harmonizing the Mode: Chord Voicings

It is important to know the chords of any key, scale, or mode in order to have a full understanding of the soloing possibilities. Following are chords constructed from the C Ionian mode. Be sure you can transpose them to all the other keys. The chord types remain constant in every key.

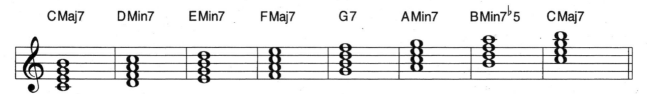

Here are two possibilities for voicing the harmonies for this mode. The first is for A♭ Ionian and the second is for G Ionian. Read through them from left to right.

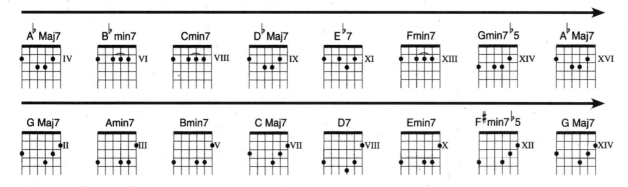

Using the Mode: Improvisation

Use the Ionian mode when improvising over any of the chords constructed from the harmonized Ionian mode. Also, use the Ionian mode built on the root of any of the following chord types: Major, Maj6, Maj7, Maj9, Maj13, Maj6/9, Maj7/6. On the following page are some sample progressions to practice improvising over using the Ionian mode, plus a couple of sample licks.

1. F Ionian

FMaj7   Gmin7

2. G Ionian

GMaj7   Emin7   Amin7   D7

3. B♭ Ionian, E♭ Ionian, A♭ Ionian, D♭ Ionian

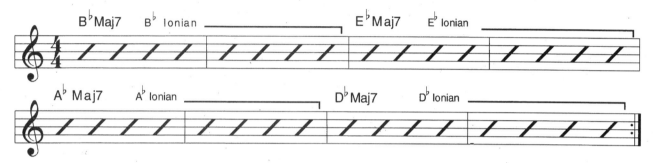

B♭Maj7   B♭ Ionian   E♭Maj7   E♭ Ionian

A♭ Maj7   A♭ Ionian   D♭Maj7   D♭ Ionian

4. C Ionian

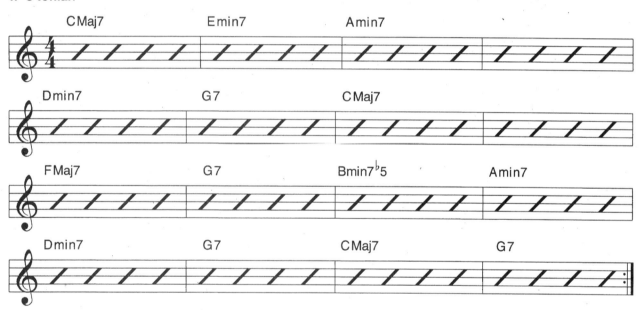

CMaj7   Emin7   Amin7

Dmin7   G7   CMaj7

FMaj7   G7   Bmin7♭5   Amin7

Dmin7   G7   CMaj7   G7

Licks

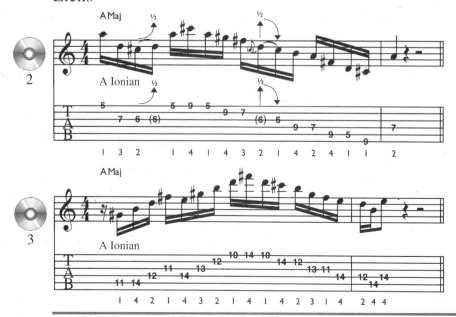

Melodic Patterns: For Practice

G Ionian

A Ionian

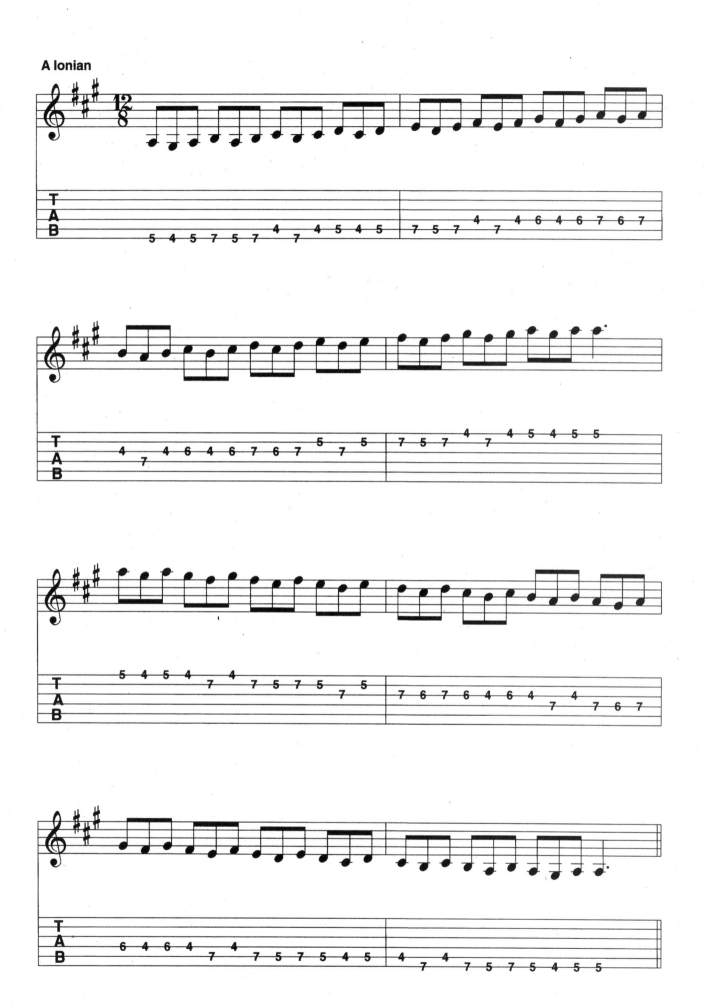

Following is a song chart for "C Ionian Backing Track." Each chapter concludes with a similar backing track so you can practice soloing using all of the strategies and information you learned in that chapter.

C Ionian Backing Track
4

Moderate Rock ♩ = 94
No drums or guitar

Play 14 times (total)
With drums and guitar

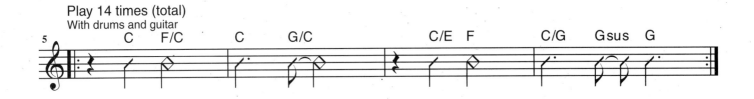

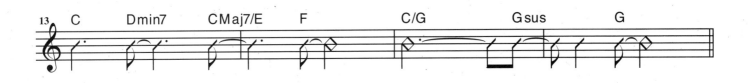

Play 8 times (total)

THE DORIAN MODE

In Every Key on Single Strings

The Dorian mode is a minor-type scale that is built on the second degree of any major scale and therefore shares the same key signature. Here is the mode in all the keys. The keys are arranged in a cycle of fourths.

C Dorian

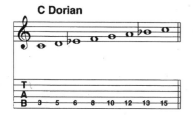

F Dorian

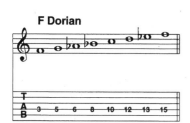

B♭ Dorian

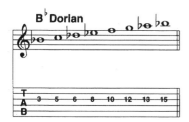

E♭ Dorian

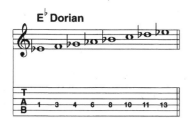

A♭ Dorian

D♭ Dorian

G♭ Dorian

G♭ and F♯ are enharmonically equivalent. The notes sound the same but are named differently.

F♯ Dorian

B Dorian

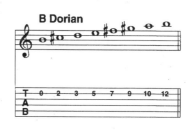

E Dorian

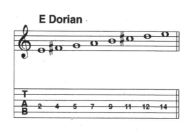

A Dorian

D Dorian

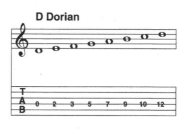

G Dorian

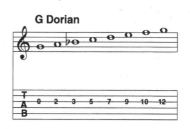

Perspective #1: Finding the Half Steps

The formula for the Dorian mode is 1–1/2–1–1–1–1/2–1. The half steps appear between steps 2 and 3, and between 6 and 7. Here is the D Dorian mode along each string.

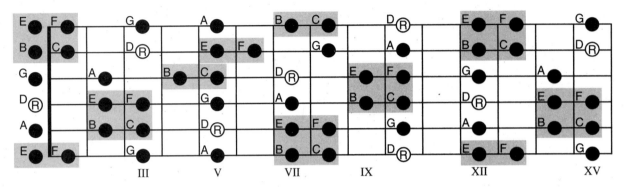

Perspective #2: Thinking in a Parent Key

To use this method effectively you must know what the ii chord is in every major key. For instance, if the chord is Fmin7 and you want to use Dorian sounds, you would ask yourself, "in what key is Fmin7 the ii chord?" The answer is, of course, E♭ Major.

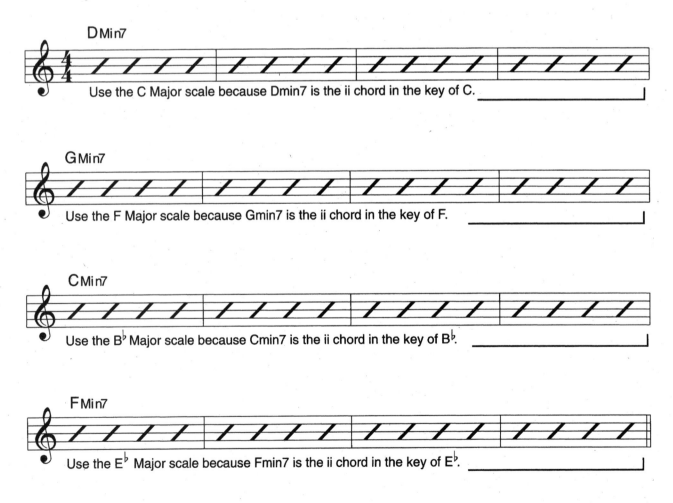

DMin7

Use the C Major scale because Dmin7 is the ii chord in the key of C.

GMin7

Use the F Major scale because Gmin7 is the ii chord in the key of F.

CMin7

Use the B♭ Major scale because Cmin7 is the ii chord in the key of B♭.

FMin7

Use the E♭ Major scale because Fmin7 is the ii chord in the key of E♭.

Perspective #3: Altering a Scale

By flatting the third and seventh degrees of any major scale, we construct the parallel Dorian mode.

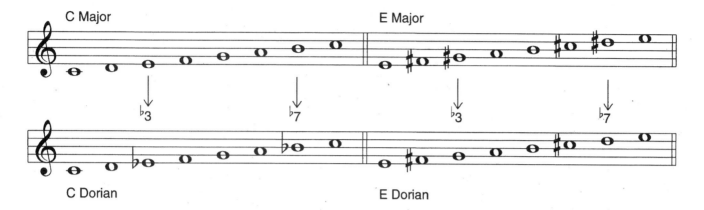

Perspective #4: In Relation to a Chord's Root

You can locate the Dorian mode by thinking of the major key signature that lies a major second below the chord's root. If you wanted to use A Dorian against an Amin7 chord, or an A "power chord," you would think in the key of G Major, because G lies a major second below the root of an A chord.

○ = root
■ = first note of the related major scale

If you were improvising against either of these chords, the Dorian mode could be thought of as the major scale that begins on this note (G).

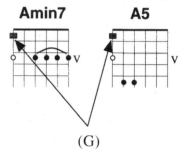

(G)

If you were improvising against either of these chords, the Dorian mode could be thought of as the major scale that begins on this note (C).

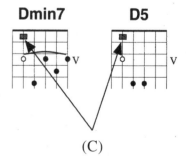

(C)

If you were improvising against either of these chords, the Dorian mode could be thought of as the major scale that begins on this note (F).

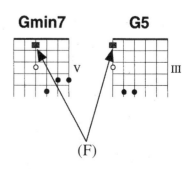

(F)

Perspective #5: Adjusting Key Signatures

You can deduce the proper key signature for a specific Dorian mode by dropping a flat or adding a sharp to the minor key signature based on the root of the chord. For D Dorian, you would think the following: "The chord is Dmin7. The key of D minor has one flat. If the flat is removed the key signature becomes C Major." Playing a C Major will create a D Dorian sound. If the chord is Bmin7: "The Key of B Minor has two sharps. Add another sharp and the key is A Major." Playing in A Major will create B Dorian sounds.

Fingerings: The Mode in Six Closed Positions

Here are six fingerings for the Dorian mode in the key of D. Practice the mode in every key.

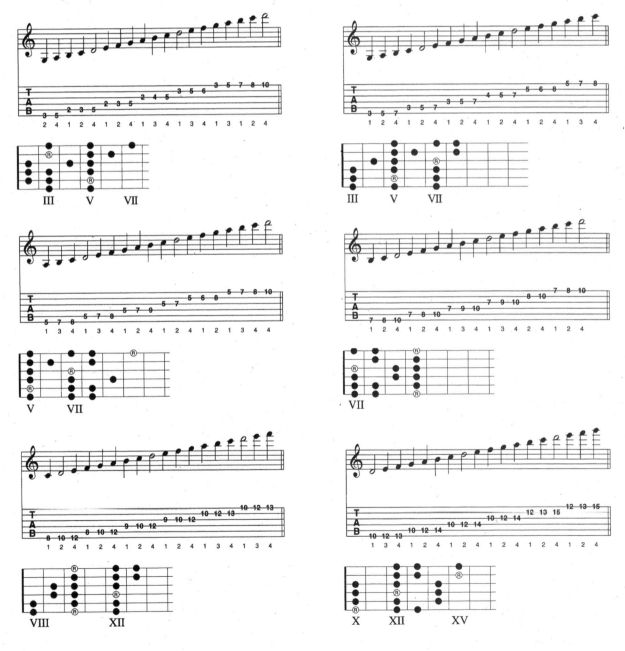

Open Position Fingerings: In Every Key

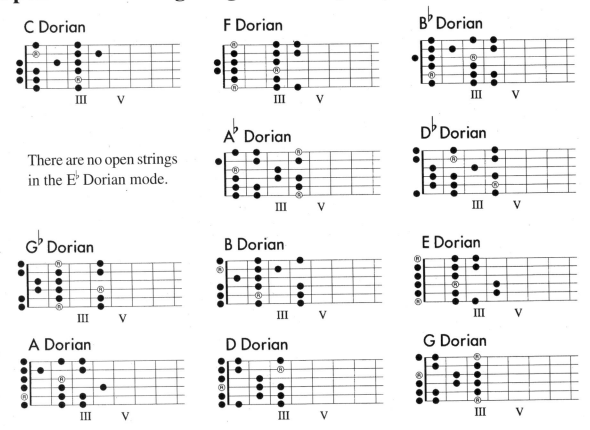

There are no open strings in the E♭ Dorian mode.

Harmonizing the Mode: Chord Voicings

These are chords constructed from the D Dorian mode. Be sure you can transpose them to all the other keys. The chord types remain constant in every key.

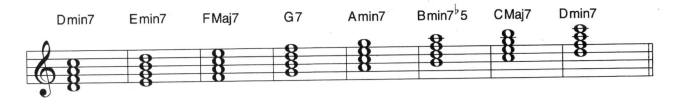

Here are two possibilities for voicing the harmonies for this mode. The first is for D Dorian and the second is for G Dorian. Read through them both from left to right.

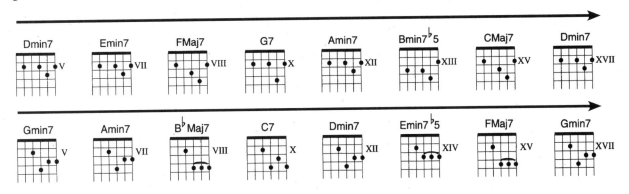

Using the Mode: Improvisation

Use the Dorian mode when improvising over any of the chords constructed from the harmonized Dorian mode. Also, use the Dorian mode built on the root of any of the following chord types: 1) minor, min6, min7, min6/9, min9, min11, min13 when functioning as a i, ii or iv harmony; 2) over a min7sus; 3) starting on the root of unaltered dominant chords and the dominant 7#9; 4) starting on the root, 4th, 5th or 7th of dominant 7th suspended chords; and 5) starting on the root, 3rd, 4th or 7th of *quartal harmonies* (chords based on perfect 4ths rather than 3rds). Below are some sample progressions to practice improvising over using the Dorian mode, followed by a couple of sample Dorian licks.

1. D Dorian

Dmin7   Emin7   Amin7   Dmin7   Emin7   Amin7

2. C Dorian

Cmin9   Dmin7   Cmin7   Dmin7

3. A Dorian

A7#9

4. G, C, D, or F Dorian

G7sus

5. C, E♭, F or B♭ Dorian

C4

Licks

Melodic Patterns: For Practice

F Dorian

(F Dorian Continued)

D Dorian

D Dorian Backing Track

THE PHRYGIAN MODE

In Every Key on Single Strings

The Phrygian mode is a minor-type scale that is built upon the third degree of any major scale and therefore shares the same key signature. Here is the mode in all the keys, arranged in a cycle of fourths.

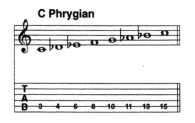

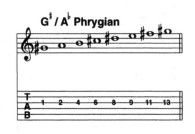

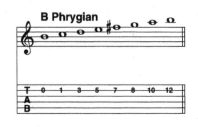

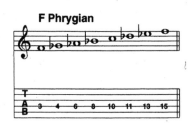

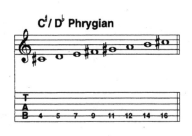

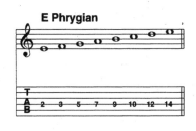

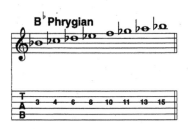

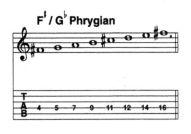

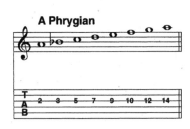

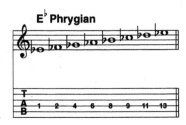

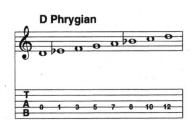

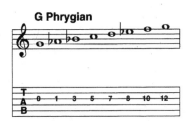

Perspective #1: Finding the Half Steps

The formula for the Phrygian mode is 1/2–1–1–1–1/2–1–1. The half steps occur between steps one and two, and five and six. Here is how the G Phrygian mode looks along each string. Study the Phrygian mode on all strings.

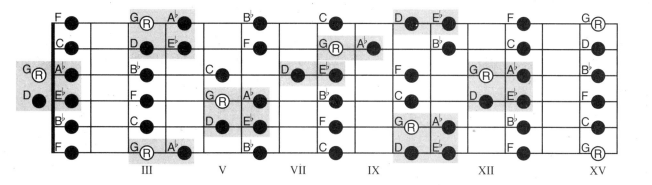

Perspective #2: Thinking in a Parent Key

Minor chords function as ii, iii or vi chords in major keys. The Phrygian mode corresponds to the iii chord. If you desired Phrygian sounds against a Bmin7 chord, you would ask yourself, "in what key is Bmin7 the iii chord?" The answer would be the key of G Major.

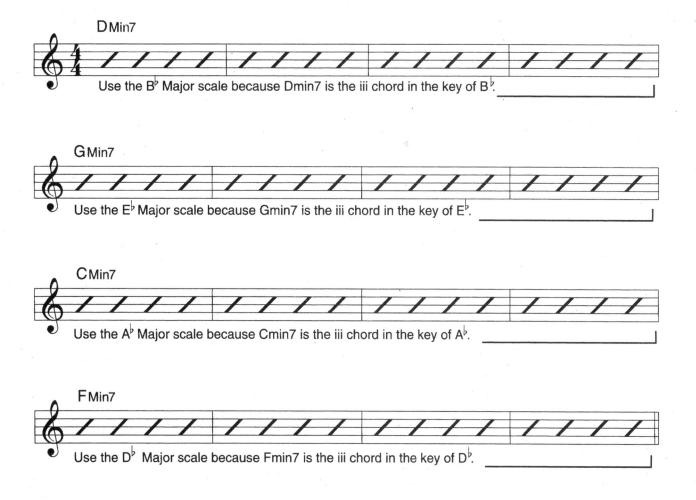

DMin7

Use the B♭ Major scale because Dmin7 is the iii chord in the key of B♭.

GMin7

Use the E♭ Major scale because Gmin7 is the iii chord in the key of E♭.

CMin7

Use the A♭ Major scale because Cmin7 is the iii chord in the key of A♭.

FMin7

Use the D♭ Major scale because Fmin7 is the iii chord in the key of D♭.

Perspective #3: Altering a Scale

The Phrygian mode is produced by flatting the second, third, sixth, and seventh degrees of the major scale. Another, possibly simpler, way would be to flat the second degree of the natural minor scale.

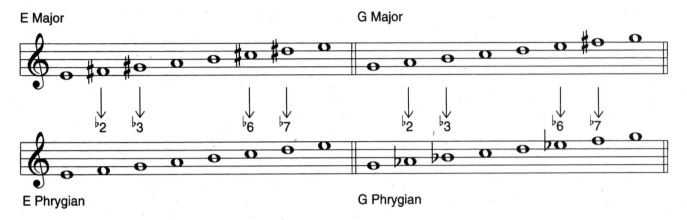

Perspective #4: In Relation to a Chord's Root

You can locate the Phrygian mode by thinking of the major key signature that lies a major third below the root of a minor chord. If you wanted to use D Phrygian against a Dmin7 chord, you would "think" in the key of B♭ Major because B♭ lies a major third below the root of the Dmin7 chord.

o = root
■ = first note of the related major scale

If you were soloing over these chords, the Phrygian mode could be thought of as the major scale that begins on this note (B♭).

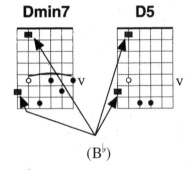

If you were improvising against either of these chords, the Phrygian mode could be thought of as the major scale that begins on this note (A♭).

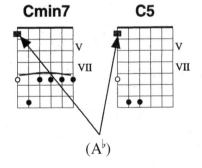

If you were improvising against either of these chords, the Phrygian mode could be thought of as the major scale that begins on this note (F).

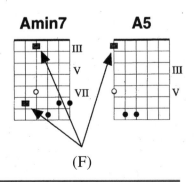

Perspective #5: Adjusting Key Signatures

You can deduce the proper key signature for a specific Phrygian mode by subtracting a sharp or adding a flat to a minor key signature based on the root of the chord. What key corresponds to C♯ Phrygian? The chord is C♯min7. The key of C♯ Minor has four sharps. By subtracting a sharp, you are now in the key of A Major. Playing in A Major puts you in C♯ Phrygian. What key corresponds to B♭ Phrygian? Perhaps the chord is B♭min7. The key of B♭ Minor has five flats. By adding a flat, you are now in G♭ Major. Playing in G♭ Major puts you in B♭ Phrygian.

Fingerings: The Mode in Six Closed Positions

Here are six fingerings for the Phrygian mode in the key of E. Practice the mode in every key!

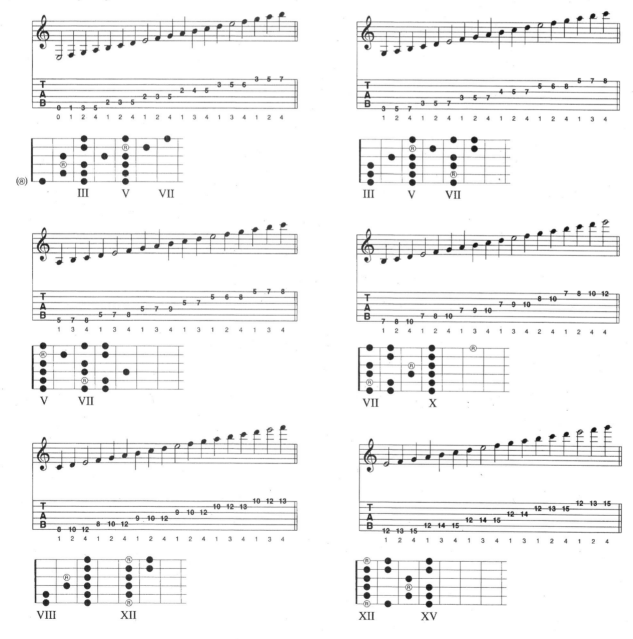

Open Position Fingerings: In Every Key

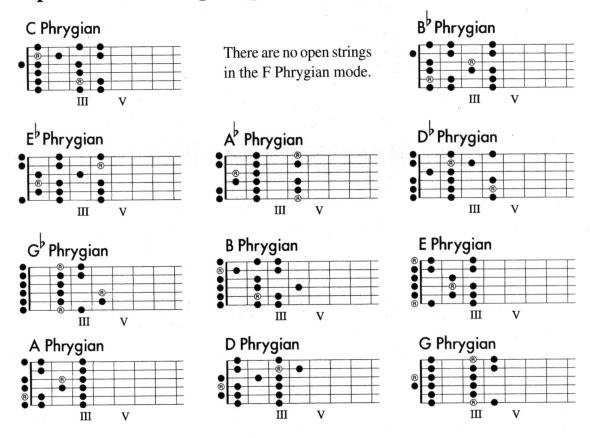

There are no open strings in the F Phrygian mode.

Harmonizing the Mode: Chord Voicings

These are the chords constructed from the E Phrygian mode. You should be comfortable with them in all twelve keys. The chord types remain constant in every key.

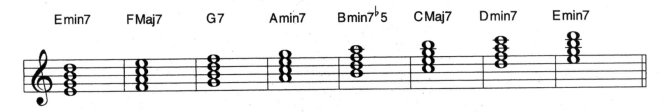

Here are two possibilities for voicing the harmonies for this mode. The first is for F# Phrygian and the second is for B♭ Phrygian. Read through them from left to right.

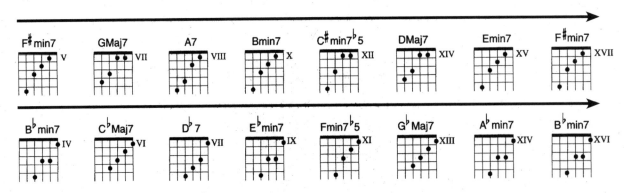

Using the Mode: Improvisation

The Phrygian mode works well over the following: 1) any of the chords in the harmonized Phrygian mode; 2) starting on the root of min7 chords in vamp situations or progressions that modulate to temporary minor key centers; 3) in minor progressions where the II chord is a Maj7 chord; and 4) starting on the root of min7$\flat$9 chords. Below are some sample Phrygian progressions and licks.

1. D Phrygian

Dmin7

2. G Phrygian

Gmin7   A$\flat$ Maj7   Gmin7   A$\flat$ Maj7

3. E Phrygian

Amin7   Emin7   F   G   Amin7

4. B Phrygian

CMaj7   Bmin7   Emin7   Bmin7

5. D Phrygian

Dmin7   E$\flat$Maj7   Dmin7   F7sus

Licks

Melodic Patterns: For Practice

E Phrygian

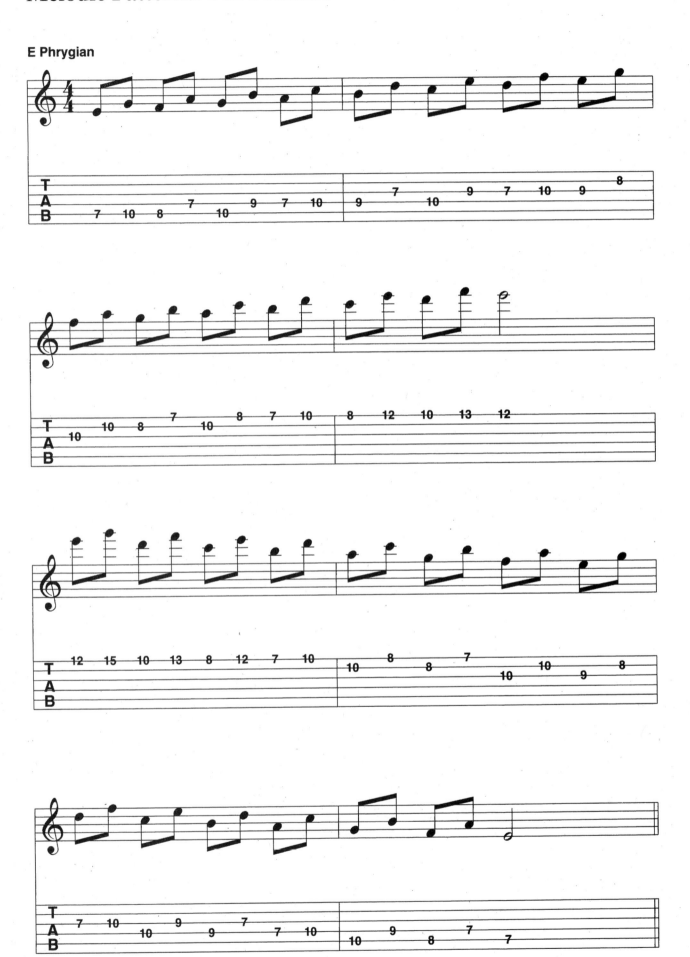

B Phrygian

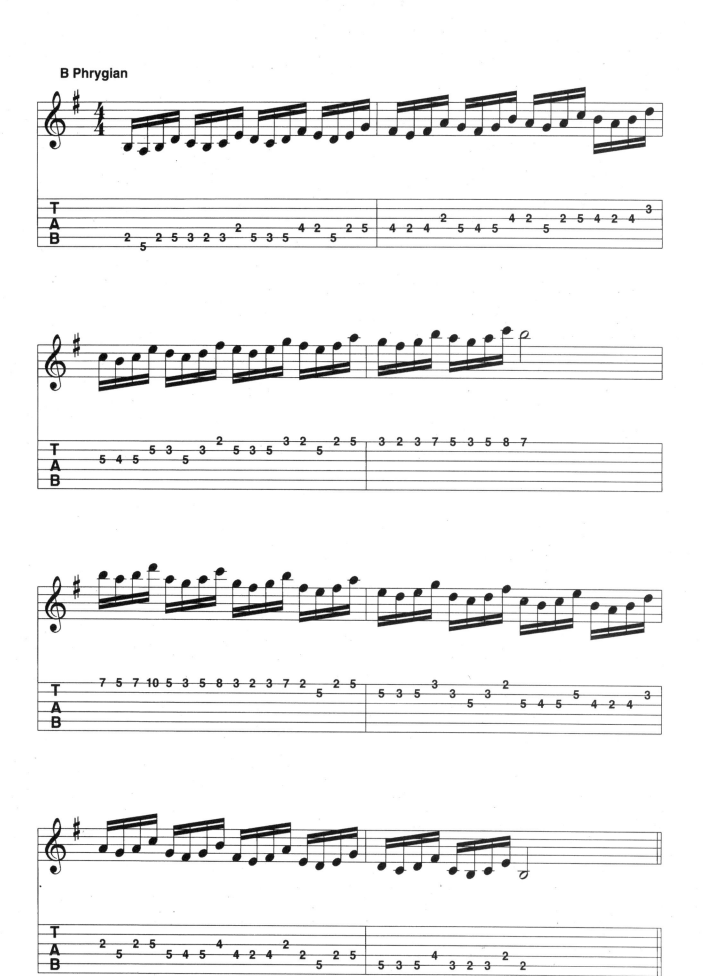

E Phrygian Backing Track

Moderate Fast Rock ♩ = 147

Intro

Play 12 times (total)

Play 4 times (total)

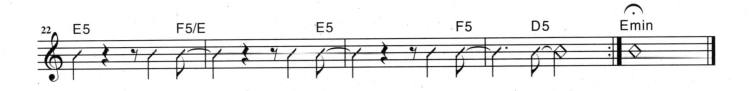

THE LYDIAN MODE

In Every Key on Single Strings

The Lydian mode is a major-type scale that is built upon the fourth degree of any major scale and shares the same key signature. Here is the mode in all the keys, arranged in a cycle of fourths.

C Lydian

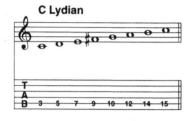

F Lydian

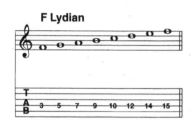

B♭ Lydian

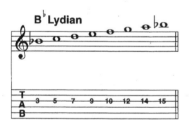

E♭ Lydian

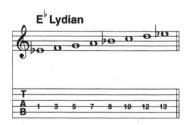

A♭ Lydian

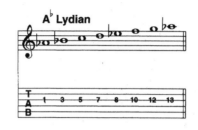

D♭ Lydian

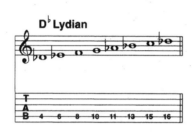

G♭ Lydian

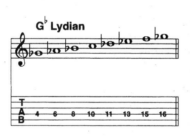

G♭ and F♯ are enharmonically equivalent. The notes sound the same but are named differently.

F♯ Lydian

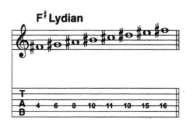

B Lydian

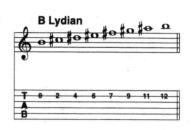

E Lydian

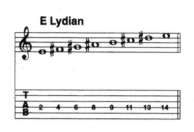

A Lydian

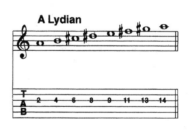

D Lydian

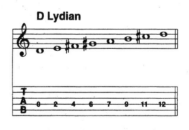

G Lydian

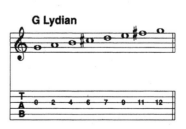

Perspective #1: Finding the Half Steps

The formula for the Lydian mode is 1–1–1–1/2–1–1–1/2. The half steps are found between steps four and five, and seven and eight. Here is how the C Lydian mode looks along each string. You should practice playing all twelve Lydian modes on each string.

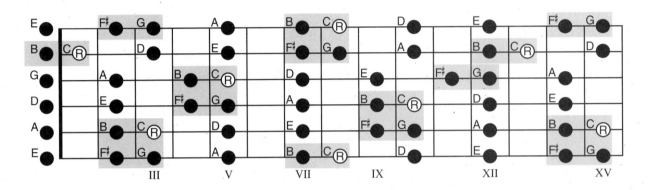

Perspective #2: Thinking in a Parent Key

Major chords function as I and IV chords in major keys. If you know what the IV chords are in every key, this approach works quite well. If the chord is a DMaj7 and you want to use Lydian sounds, ask yourself "in what key is DMaj7 the IV chord?" The answer is A Major.

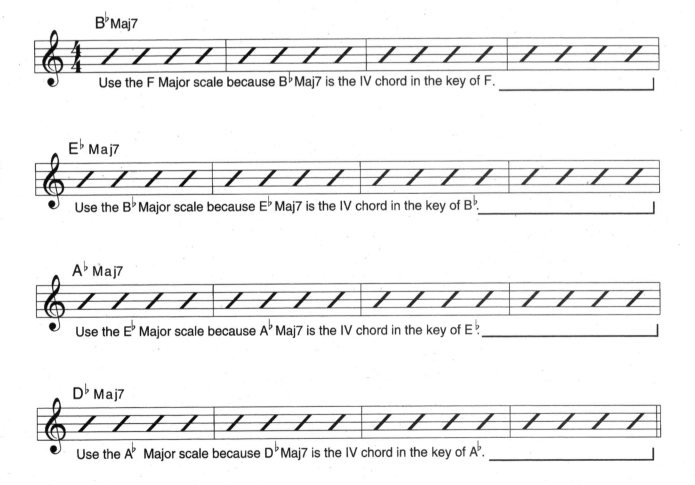

Perspective #3: Altering a Scale

The Lydian mode is produced by raising the fourth degree of any major scale.

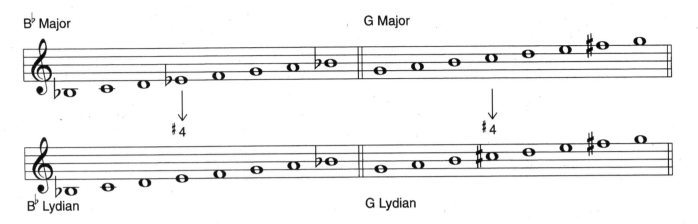

Perspective #4: In Relation to a Chord's Root

You can locate the Lydian mode by thinking of the major key signature that lies a perfect fourth below a major chord's root. If you wanted to use E Lydian over an EMaj7 chord, you would want to think in the key of B Major because B lies a perfect fourth below the root of the EMaj7 chord.

o = root
■ = first note of the related major scale

Suppose you were improvising against these chords, the Lydian mode could be thought of as the major scale that begins on this note (B).

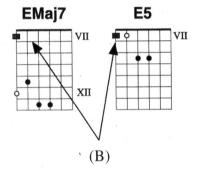

If you were improvising against either of these chords, the Lydian mode could be thought of as the major scale that begins on this note (C).

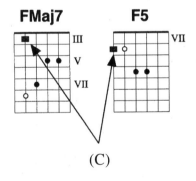

If you were improvising against either of these chords, the Lydian mode could be thought of as the major scale that begins on this note (E♭).

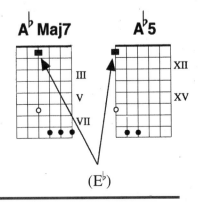

Perspective #5: Adjusting Key Signatures

You can deduce the proper key signature for a specific Lydian mode by dropping a flat or adding a sharp to the major key signature based on the root of the chord. If you are trying to figure out what key signature corresponds to D Lydian you would think the following: "The chord is DMaj7. The key of D Major has two sharps. By adding a sharp I am now in the key of A Major. Playing in the key of A Major puts me in D Lydian." What key signature corresponds to B♭ Lydian? The chord is B♭Maj7. The key of B♭ has two flats. By dropping a flat you are now in the key of F Major. Playing in the key of F Major puts you in B♭ Lydian. Practice this kind of thinking in all keys.

Fingerings: The Mode in Six Closed Positions

Here are six fingerings for the Lydian mode in the key of F. Practice the mode in every key!

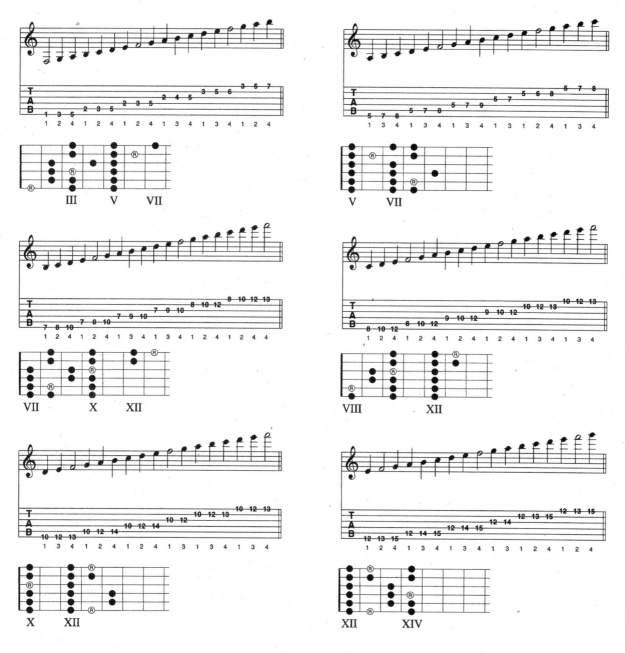

Open Position Fingerings: In Every Key

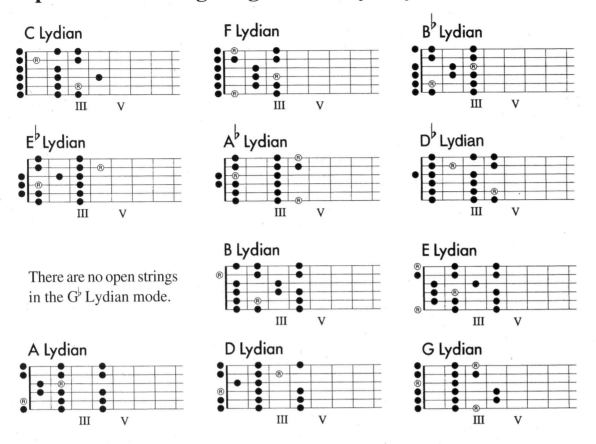

There are no open strings in the G♭ Lydian mode.

Harmonizing the Mode: Chord Voicings

These are the chords constructed from the F Lydian mode. You should be comfortable with them in all twelve keys. The chord types remain constant in every key.

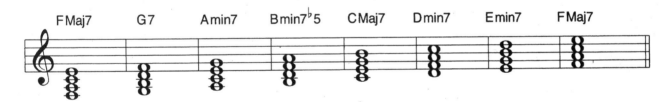

FMaj7   G7   Amin7   Bmin7♭5   CMaj7   Dmin7   Emin7   FMaj7

Here are two possibilities for voicing the harmonies for this mode. The first is for C Lydian, and the second is for E♭ Lydian. Read through them from left to right.

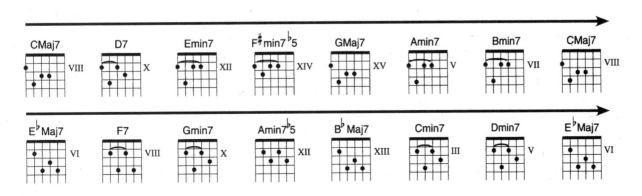

Using the Mode: Improvisation

The Lydian mode works well over the following harmonies: 1) any of the chords in the harmonized Lydian mode; 2) starting on the root of Major, Maj6, Maj9, Maj13, Maj6/9 and Maj7/6 chords; and 3) starting on the root of Maj7#11, Maj9#11 and Maj7♭5 chords. Following are some sample Lydian progressions and licks.

1. B♭ Lydian

B♭ Maj7 · A min7 · G min7 · F Maj7

2. F Lydian

F Maj9

3. D Lydian

D Maj7#11 · C#min7

4. C Lydian, then E♭ Lydian

C Maj7#11 · E♭ Maj7#11

5. G Lydian

G Maj7#11 · B min7 · E min7 · B min7

Licks

Melodic Patterns: For Practice

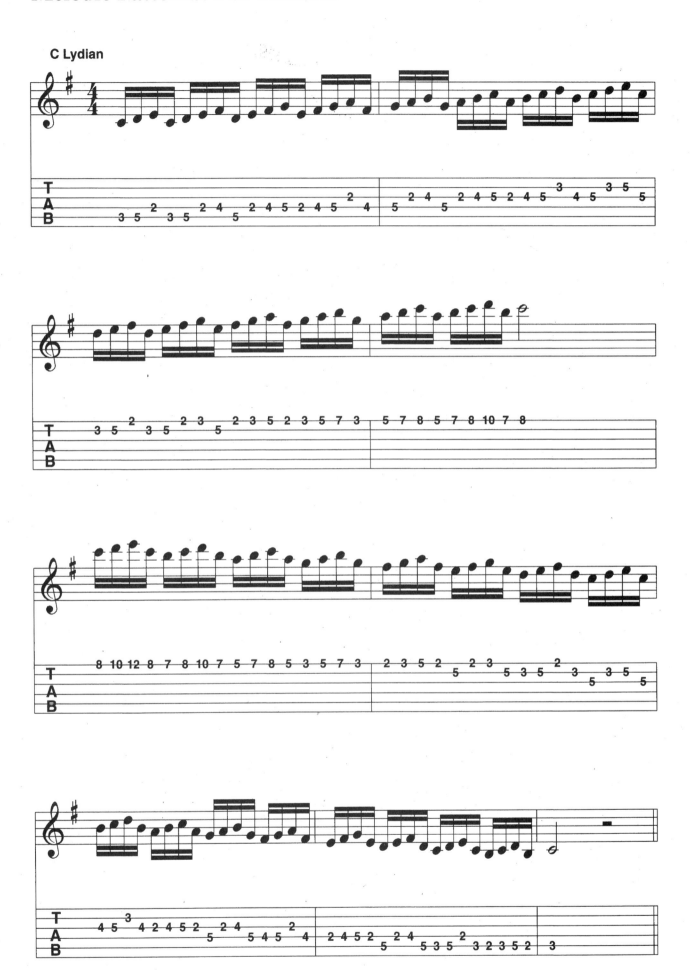

C Lydian

G Lydian

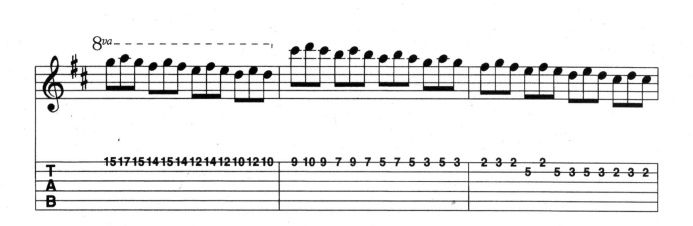

F Lydian Backing Track

13

THE MIXOLYDIAN MODE

In Every Key on Single Strings

The Mixolydian mode is a dominant-type scale that is built upon the fifth degree of any major scale and therefore shares the same key signature. Here is the mode in all the keys, arranged by the cycle of fourths.

C Mixolydian

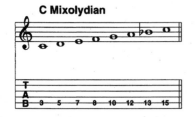

A♭ Mixolydian

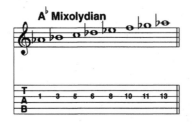

B Mixolydian

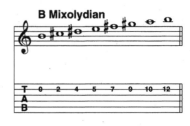

F Mixolydian

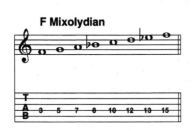

D♭ Mixolydian

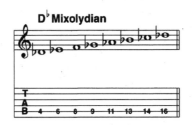

E Mixolydian

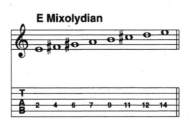

B♭ Mixolydian

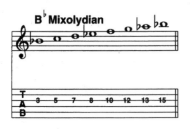

G♭ Mixolydian

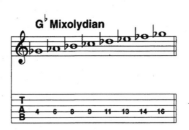

A Mixolydian

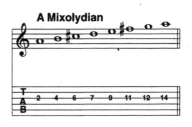

E♭ Mixolydian

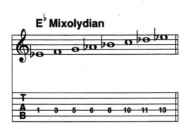

G♭ and F# are enharmonically equivalent. The notes sound the same but are named differently.

D Mixolydian

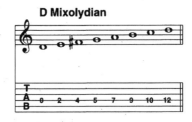

F# Mixolydian

G Mixolydian

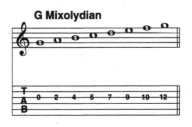

Perspective #1: Finding the Half Steps

The formula for the Mixolydian mode is 1–1–1/2–1–1–1/2–1. The half steps occur between steps three and four, and six and seven. The F Mixolydian mode is shown below along the six individual strings. You should practice all twelve Mixolydian modes on each string.

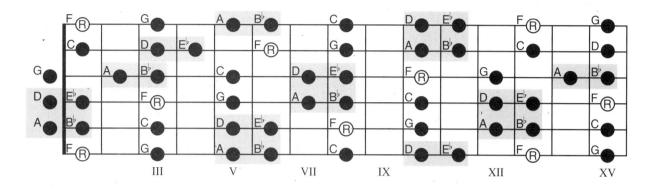

Perspective #2: Thinking in a Parent Key

Dominant chords function as V chords in major keys. You must know what the V chords are in every key to use this approach. If the chord you are improvising on is G7 and you want to use the Mixolydian mode, you would use the C Major scale because G7 is the V chord in the key of C.

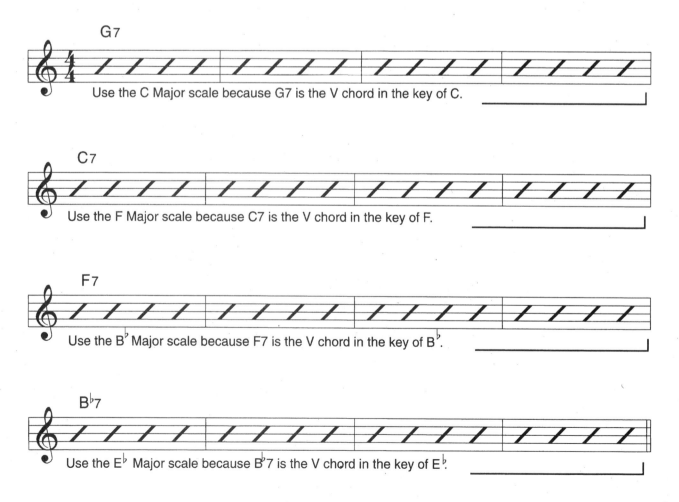

Perspective #3: Altering a Scale

The Mixolydian mode is produced by lowering the seventh degree of any major scale.

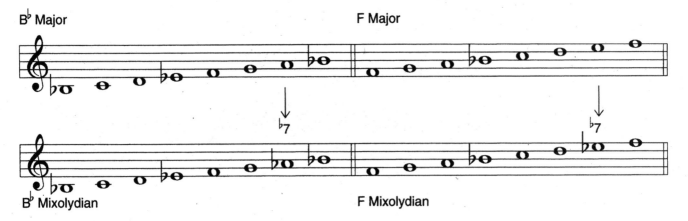

Perspective #4: In Relation to a Chord's Root

You locate the Mixolydian mode by thinking of the major key signature that lies a perfect fifth below a dominant chord's root. If you wanted to use A Mixolydian against an A7 chord, you would think in the key of D because D lies a perfect fifth below the root of the A7 chord.

o = root
■ = first note of the related major scale

Suppose you were improvising against these chords, the Mixolydian mode could be thought of as the major scale that begins on this note (G).

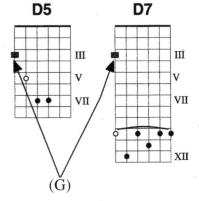

If you were improvising against either of these chords, the Mixolydian mode could be thought of as the major scale that begins on this note (B♭).

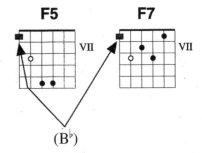

If you were improvising against either of these chords, the Mixolydian mode could be thought of as the major scale that begins on this note (F).

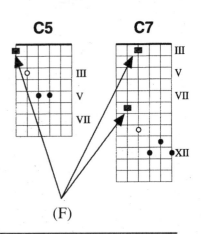

Perspective #5: Adjusting Key Signatures

You can deduce the proper key signature for a specific Mixolydian mode by subtracting a sharp or adding a flat to the major key signature based on the root of the chord. If you wanted to figure out what key signature corresponds to E Mixolydian, you would think the following: "The chord is E7. The key of E Major has four sharps. By subtracting a sharp, I am now in the key of A Major. Playing in the key of A Major puts me in E Mixolydian." What key signature corresponds to A♭ Mixolydian? The chord is A♭7. The key of A♭ Major has four flats. By adding a flat we are now in the key of D♭ Major. Playing D♭ Major puts us in A♭ Mixolydian.

Fingerings: The Mode in Six Closed Positions

Here are six fingerings for the Mixolydian mode in the key of G. Practice the mode in every key!

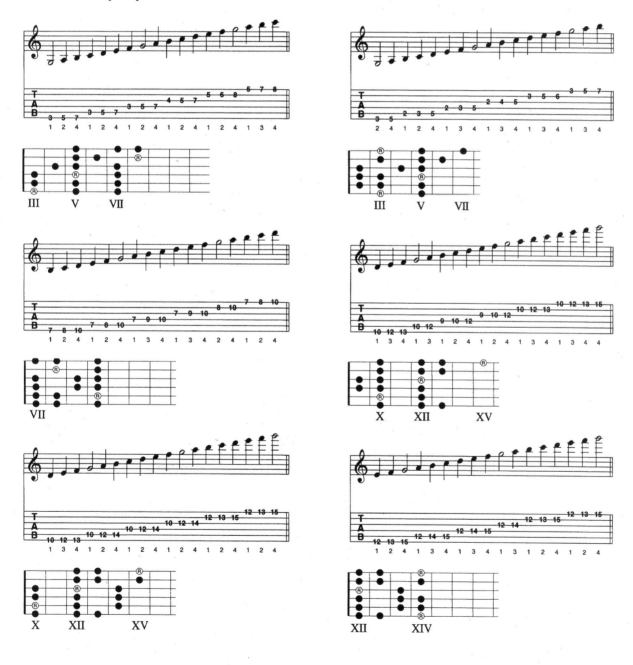

Open Position Fingerings: In Every Key

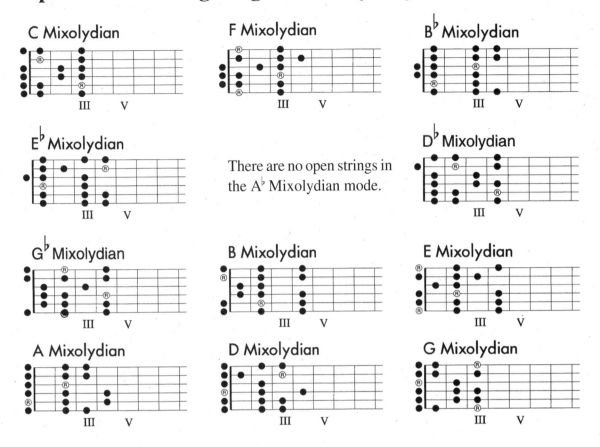

There are no open strings in the A♭ Mixolydian mode.

Harmonizing the Mode: Chord Voicings

These are the chords constructed from the harmonized Mixolydian mode in G. You should be comfortable with them in all twelve keys. The chord types remain constant in every key.

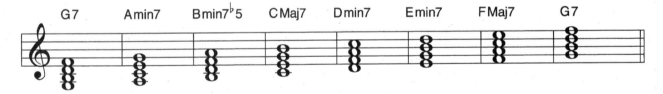

Here are two possibilities for voicing the harmonies for this mode. The first is for D Mixolydian and the second is for B Mixolydian. Read through them from left to right.

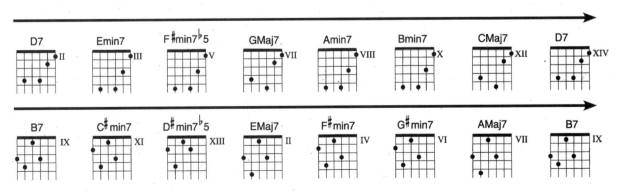

Using the Mode: Improvisation

The Mixolydian mode works well over the following: 1) any of the chords in the harmonized Mixolydian mode; and 2) starting on the root of dominant 7th, 9th, 11th and 13th chords where no alterations are present. Following are some sample Mixolydian progressions and licks.

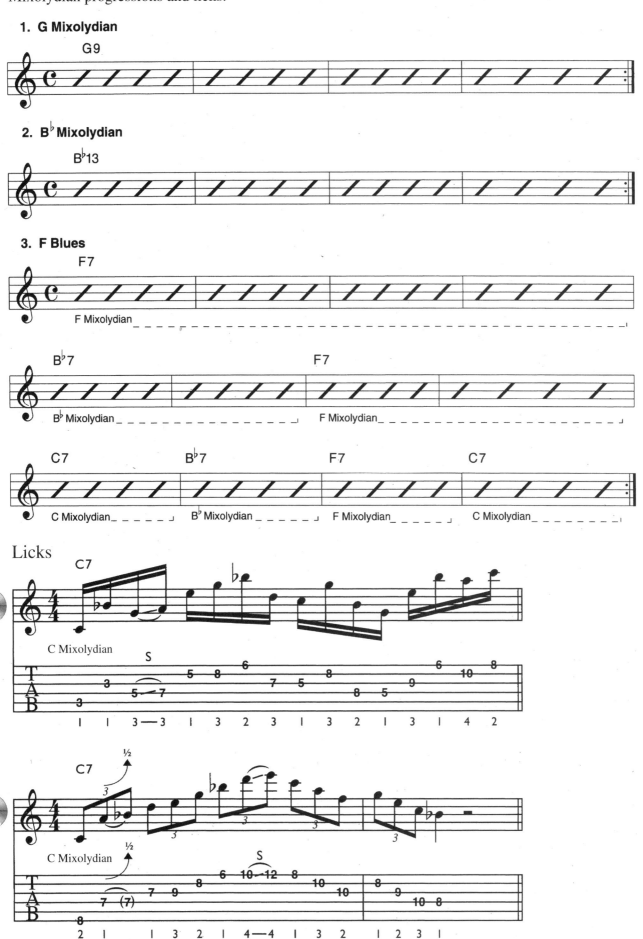

1. G Mixolydian

G9

2. B♭ Mixolydian

B♭13

3. F Blues

F7

F Mixolydian

B♭7   F7

B♭ Mixolydian   F Mixolydian

C7   B♭7   F7   C7

C Mixolydian   B♭ Mixolydian   F Mixolydian   C Mixolydian

Licks

C7

C Mixolydian

C7

C Mixolydian

Melodic Patterns: For Practice

C Mixolydian

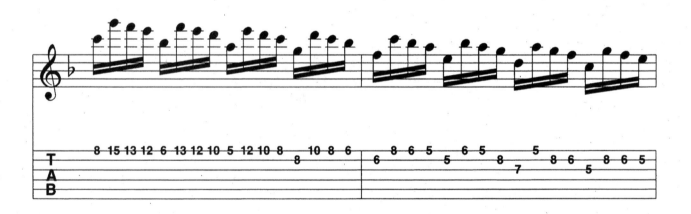

F Mixolydian

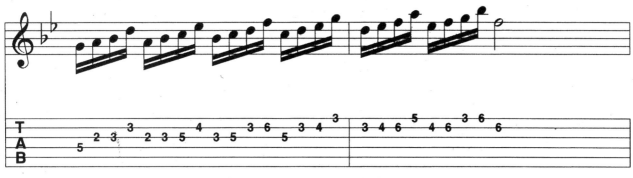

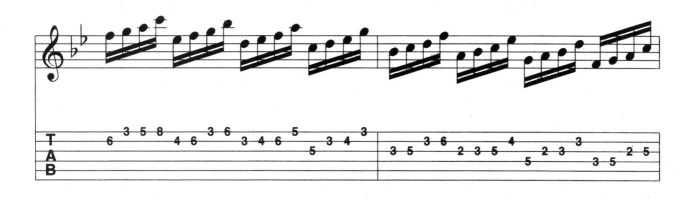

G Mixolydian Backing Track

Moderate Shuffle ♩. = 139
Intro

Play 10 times (total)

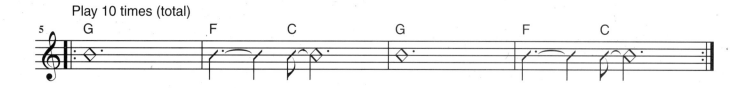

Play 8 times (total)

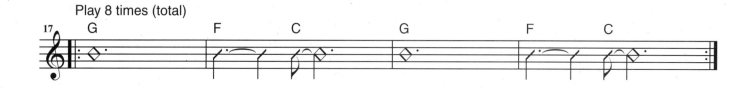

THE AEOLIAN MODE

In Every Key on Single Strings

The Aeolian mode is a minor-type scale that is built upon the sixth degree of any major scale and therefore shares the same key signature. It is also known as the natural minor scale. Here is the mode in all the keys, arranged in a cycle of fourths.

C Aeolian
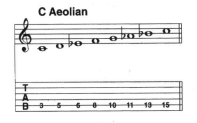

F Aeolian
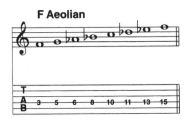

B♭ Aeolian
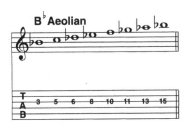

E♭ Aeolian
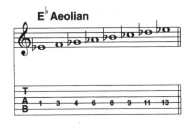

A♭ Aeolian
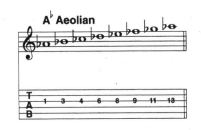

D♭ Aeolian

G♭ Aeolian
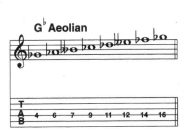

G♭ and F♯ are enharmonically equivalent. The notes sound the same but are named differently.

F♯ Aeolian
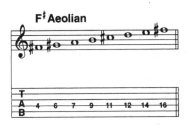

B Aeolian
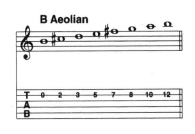

E Aeolian
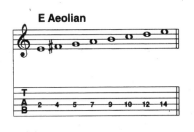

A Aeolian
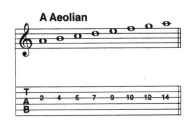

D Aeolian
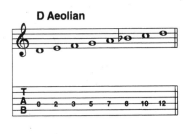

G Aeolian
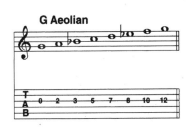

Perspective #1: Finding the Half Steps

The formula for the Aeolian mode is 1–1/2–1–1–1/2–1–1. The half steps occur between steps two and three, and five and six. The E Aeolian mode is shown below on all strings. Practice improvising in all keys using the Aeolian mode up and down each string.

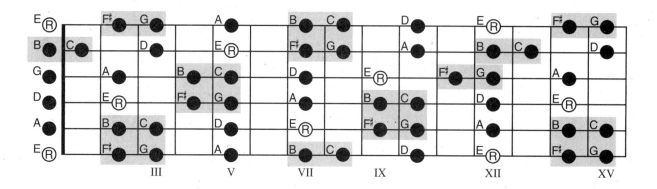

Perspective #2: Thinking in a Parent Key

Minor chords function as ii, iii, or vi chords in major keys. The Aeolian mode corresponds to vi chords. If you were improvising against a Gmin chord and you wanted to hear Aeolian sounds, you would ask yourself, "in what key is Gmin the vi chord?" The answer, of course, is B♭ Major.

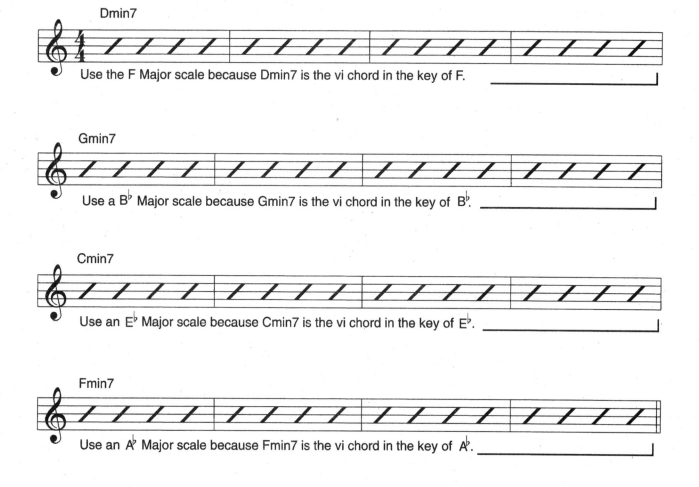

Perspective #3: Altering a Scale

The Aeolian mode is produced by lowering the third, sixth, and seventh degrees of any major scale.

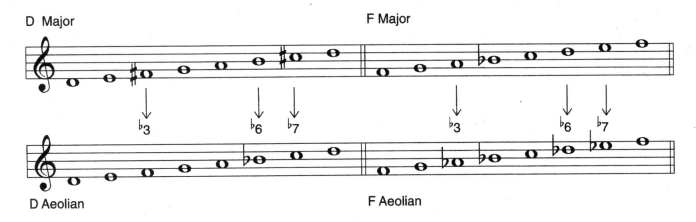

Perspective #4: In Relation to a Chord's Root

You can locate the Aeolian mode by thinking of the major key signature that lies a minor third above a minor chord's root. If you wanted to use B Aeolian against a Bmin7 chord, you would think in the key of D Major because D lies a minor third above the root of the Bmin7 chord.

○ = root
■ = first note of the related major scale

Suppose you were improvising against these chords, the Aeolian mode could be thought of as the major scale that begins on this note (C).

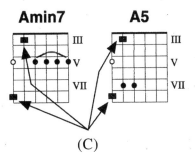

If you were improvising against either of these chords, the Aeolian mode could be thought of as the major scale that begins on this note (G).

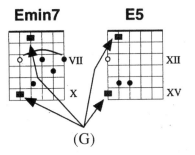

If you were improvising against either of these chords, the Aeolian mode could be thought of as the major scale that begins on this note (B♭).

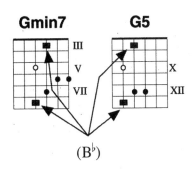

Perspective #5: Adjusting Key Signatures

The Aeolian mode corresponds exactly to the minor key signatures so no adjustments are necessary. The key signature for C Aeolian is the same as the key signature for the key of C Minor. D Aeolian's key signature is the same as the key of D Minor, etc.

Fingerings: The Mode in Six Closed Positions

Here are six fingerings for the Aeolian mode in the key of A. Practice the mode in every key!

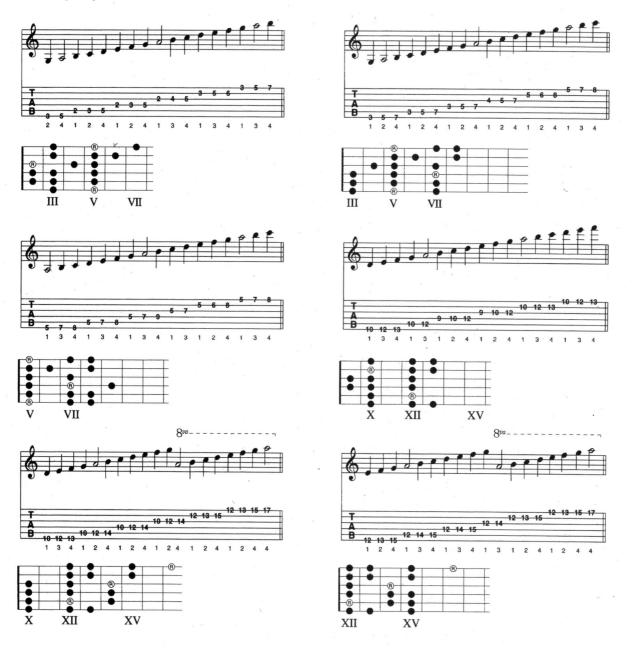

Open Position Fingerings: In Every Key

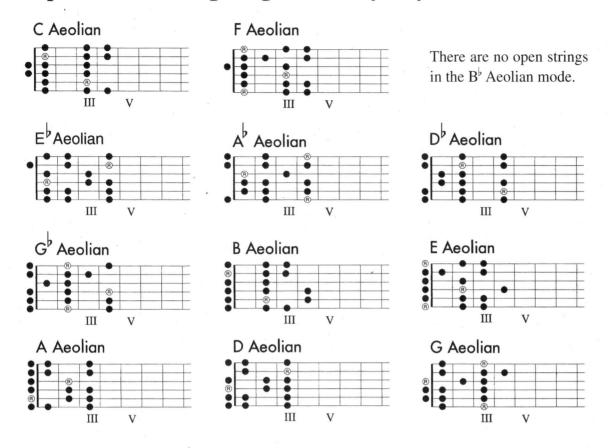

There are no open strings in the B♭ Aeolian mode.

Harmonizing the Mode: Chord Voicings

These are the chords constructed from the harmonized Aeolian mode. You should be comfortable with them in all twelve keys. The chord types remain constant in every key.

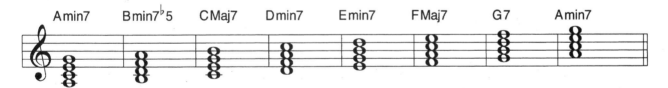

Here are two possibilities for voicing the harmonies for this mode. The first is for A Aeolian and the second is for B Aeolian. Read through them from left to right.

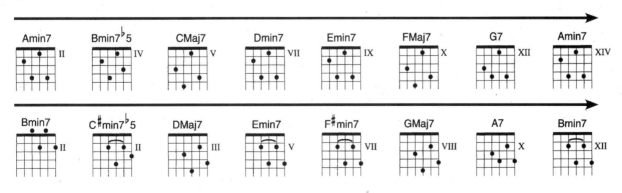

Using the Mode: Improvisation

The Aeolian mode works well over the following: 1) any of the chords in the harmonized Aeolian mode; 2) starting at the root of minor triads, min6, min7, min9, min11, min13, minadd9, and min7add11 chords; and 3) in minor chord progressions where the ii chord is a min7♭5 (half-diminished) chord. Following are some sample Aeolian progressions and licks.

Melodic Patterns: For Practice

C Aeolian

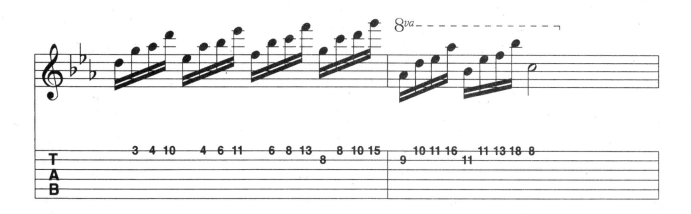

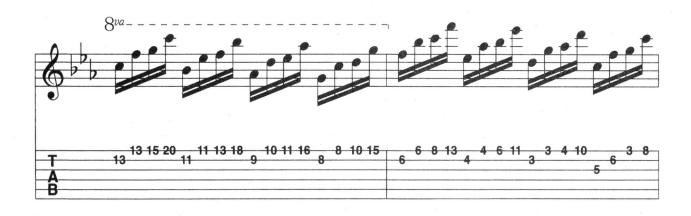

D Aeolian

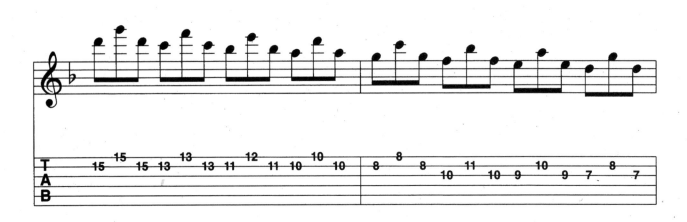

A Aeolian Backing Track

THE LOCRIAN MODE

In Every Key on Single Strings

The Locrian mode is a half-diminished scale that is built upon the seventh degree
of any major scale and therefore shares the same key signature. Here is the mode in
all the keys, arranged in a cycle of fourths.

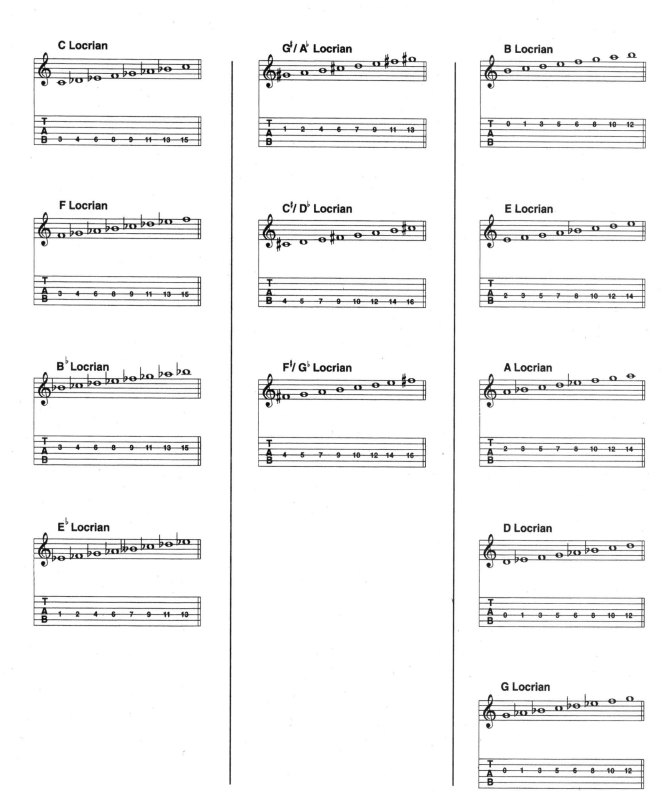

Perspective #1: Finding the Half Steps

The formula for the Locrian mode is 1/2–1–1–1/2–1–1–1. The half steps occur between steps one and two, and four and five. The A Locrian mode is shown below on all strings. Practice improvising in all keys using the Locrian mode up and down each string.

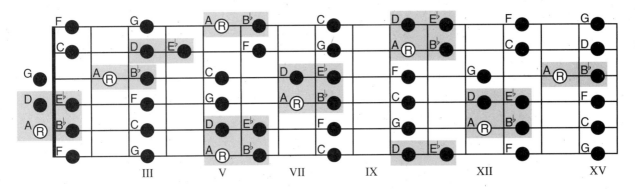

Perspective #2: Thinking in a Parent Key

Half-diminished chords (min7♭5) function as vii chords in major keys. The Locrian mode corresponds to vii chords. If you were improvising against an A half-diminished chord and you wanted to hear Locrian sounds, you would ask yourself, "in what key is Amin7♭5 the vii chord?" The answer is B♭.

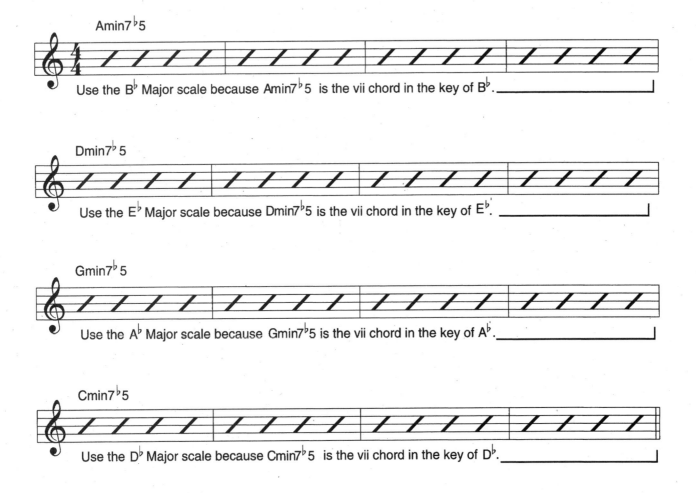

Perspective #3: Altering a Scale

The Locrian mode is produced by lowering the second, third, fifth, sixth, and seventh degrees of any major scale.

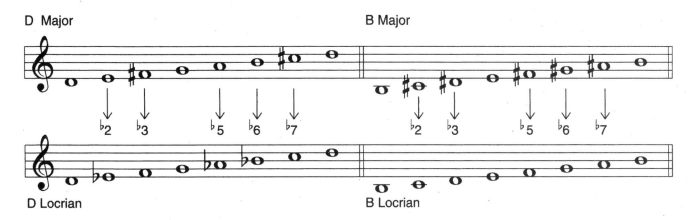

Perspective #4: In Relation to a Chord's Root

You can locate the Locrian mode by thinking of the major key signature that lies a minor second above a half-diminished (min7♭5) chord's root. If you wanted to use G Locrian against a G half-diminished chord, you would think in the key of A♭ Major because A♭ lies a minor second above the root of the G half-diminished chord.

Suppose you were improvising against this chord, the Locrian mode could be thought of as the major scale that begins on this note (E♭).

If you were improvising against this chord, the Locrian mode could be thought of as the major scale that begins on this note (F).

If you were improvising against this chord, the Locrian mode could be thought of as the major scale that begins on this note (A♭).

o = root
■ = first note of the related major scale

Dmin7♭5

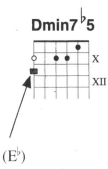

(E♭)

Emin7♭5

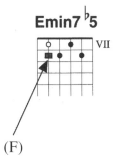

(F)

Gmin7♭5

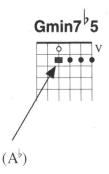

(A♭)

Perspective #5: Adjusting Key Signatures

You can deduce the proper key signature for a specific Locrian mode by adding two flats or subtracting two sharps from the minor key signature based on the root of the chord. If you wanted to figure out what key signature corresponds to D Locrian, you would think the following: "The chord is Dmin7♭5. The key of D Minor has one flat. By adding two flats, I am now in the key of E♭. Playing in E♭ Major puts me in D Locrian." Suppose you wanted to figure out the key signature for C♯ Locrian. The chord is C♯min7♭5. The key of C♯ Minor has four sharps. By subtracting two sharps we are now in the key of D Major. Playing in the key of D Major puts us in C♯ Locrian. To create E Locrian, subtract a sharp and add a flat to the key of E Minor. Practice this kind of thinking in all keys.

Fingerings: The Mode in Six Closed Positions

Here are six fingerings for the Locrian mode in the key of B. Practice the mode in every key!

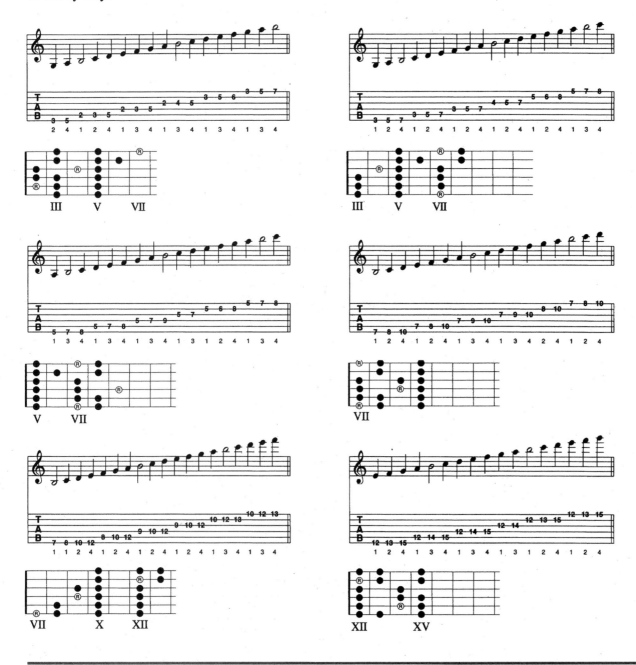

Open Position Fingerings: In Every Key

There are no open strings in the C Locrian mode.

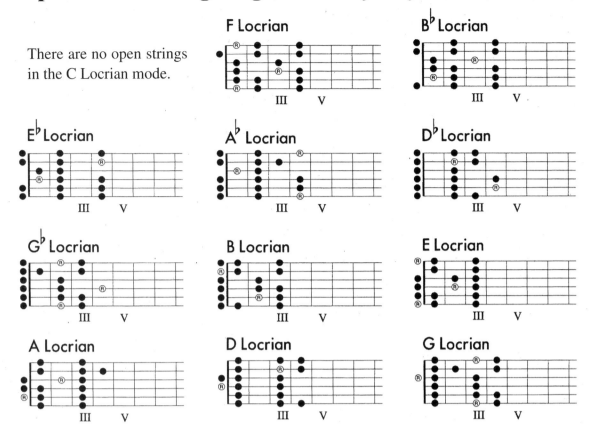

Harmonizing the Mode: Chord Voicings

These are the chords constructed from the harmonized Locrian mode in B. You should be comfortable with them in all twelve keys. The chord types remain constant in every key.

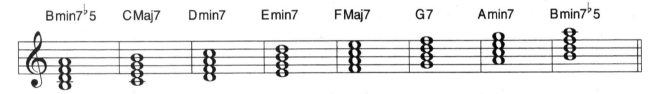

Bmin7♭5   CMaj7   Dmin7   Emin7   FMaj7   G7   Amin7   Bmin7♭5

Here are two possibilities for voicing the harmonies for this mode. The first is for A♯ Locrian, and the second is for E Locrian. Read through them from left to right.

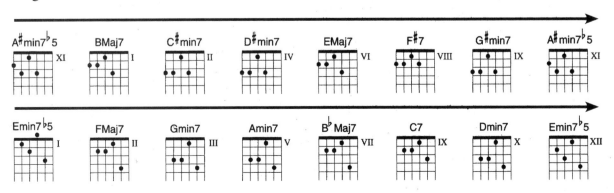

Using the Mode: Improvisation

The Locrian mode works well over the following: 1) any of the chords in the harmonized Locrian mode; and 2) starting on the root of half-diminished chords, minor triads, min6, min7, min9, min11, and min13 chords whose root is a minor third higher than the root of the Locrian mode. Following are some sample Locrian progressions and licks.

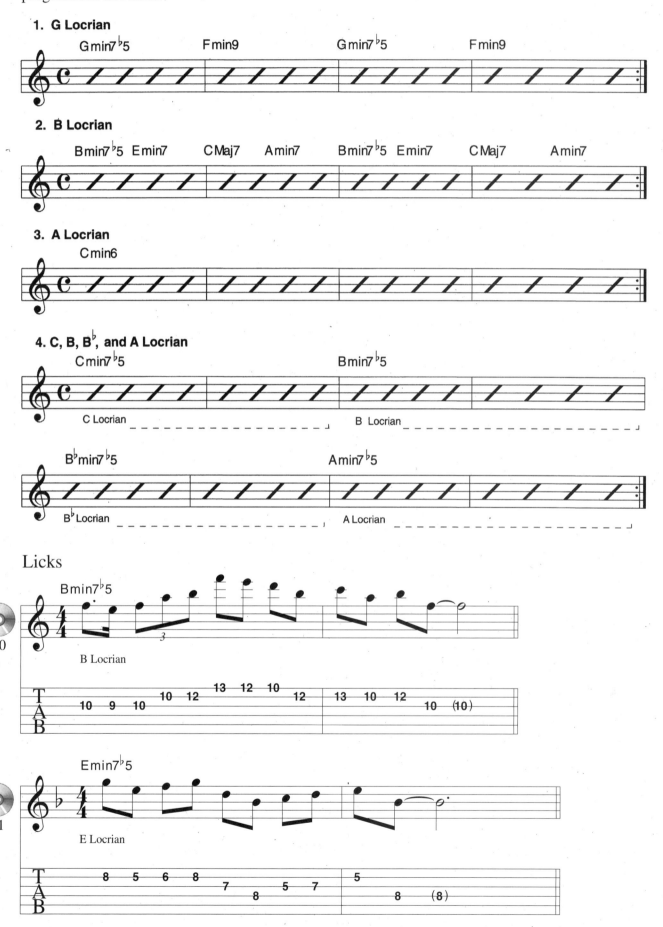

Licks

Melodic Patterns: For Practice

B Locrian

F#Locrian

B Locrian Backing Track

CONCLUDING SOLOS

This section features extended solos in real playing contexts. Each solo features one or more modes in various keys, all of which are clearly indicated in the music. Go ahead and play them as written, observing how the modes are used. Then, using these ideas as a springboard, try coming up with your own solos. Apply some of the ideas you find in this section to the backing tracks you've already worked on.

Good luck, and enjoy.

Ionian/Dorian

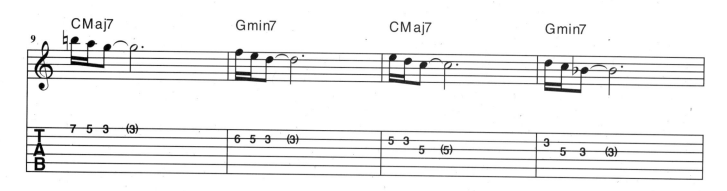

Ionian/Dorian/Phrygian

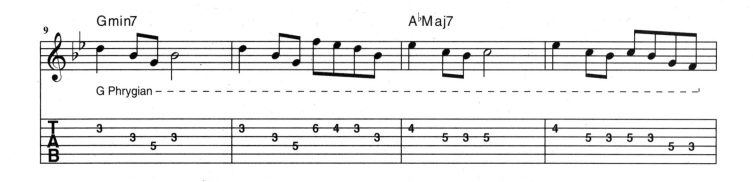

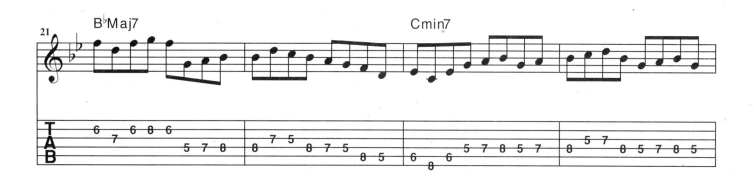

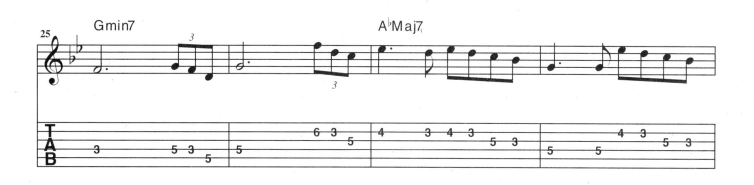

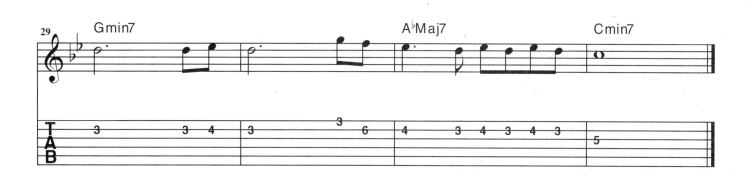

Lydian/Dorian

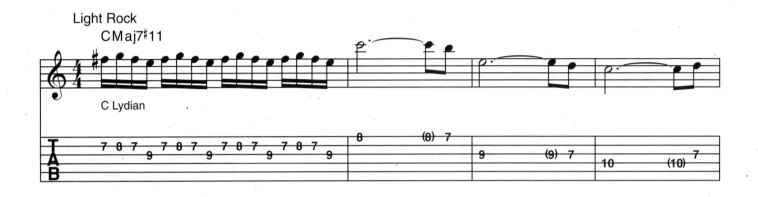

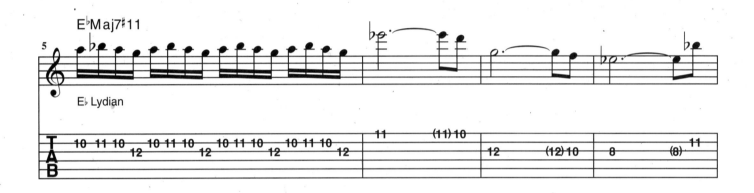

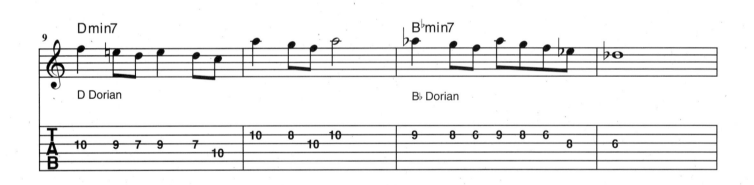

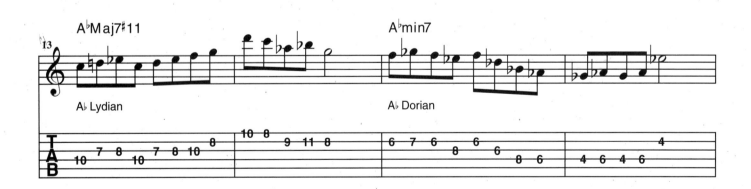

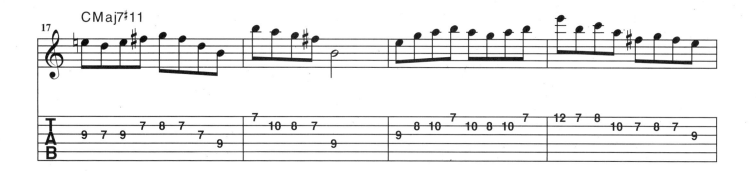

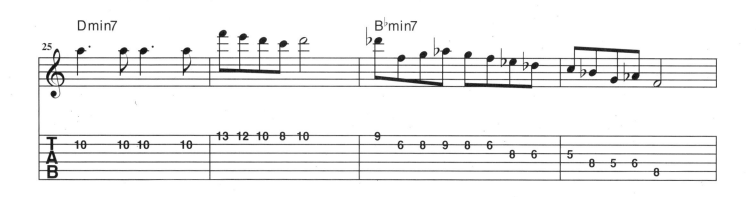

Mixolydian

Medium Tempo (Even Eighths)

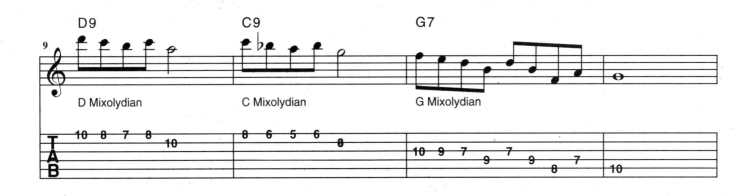

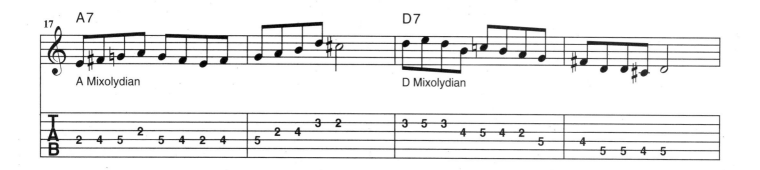

Aeolian/Mixolydian

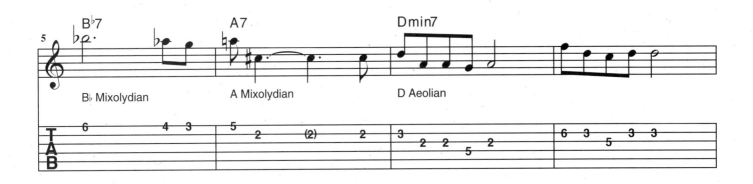

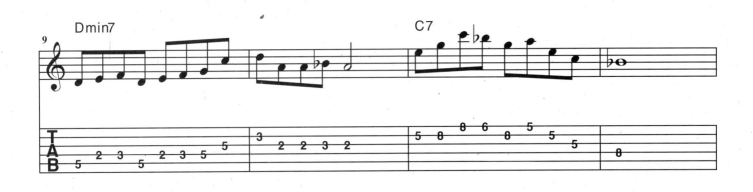

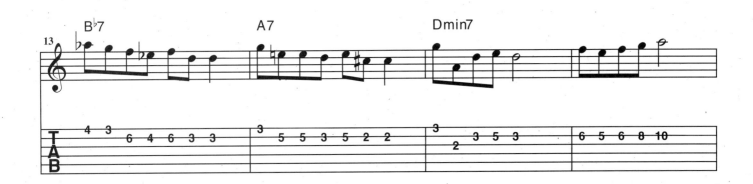

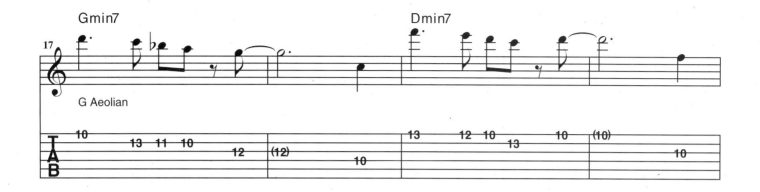

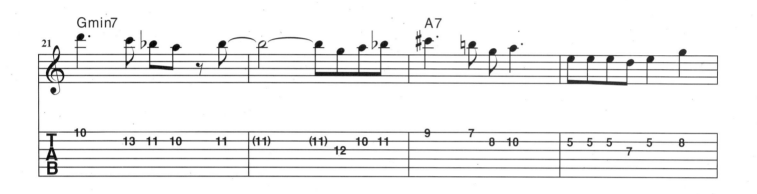

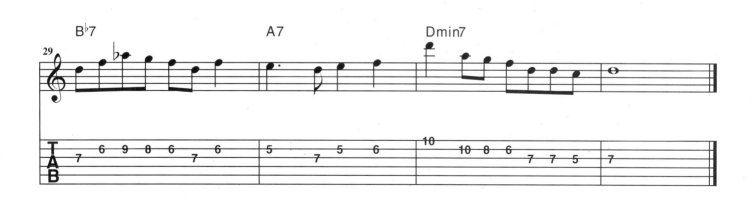

Locrian/Mixolydian/Aeolian

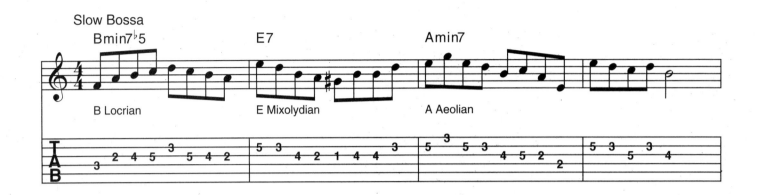

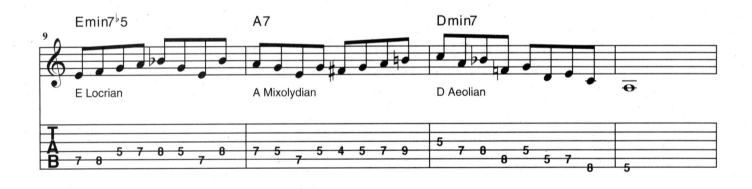

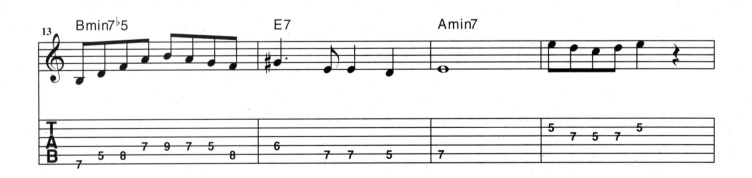

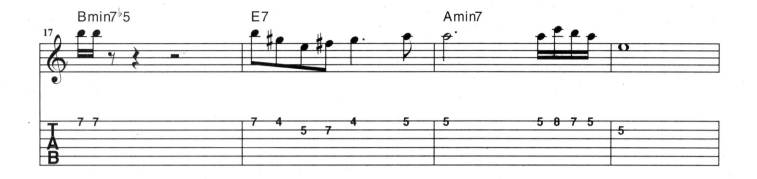

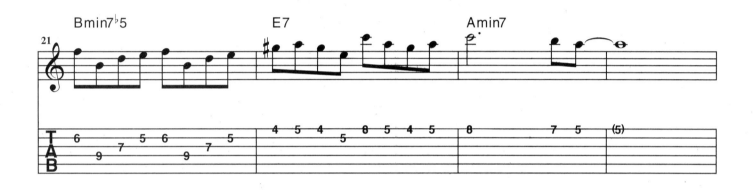

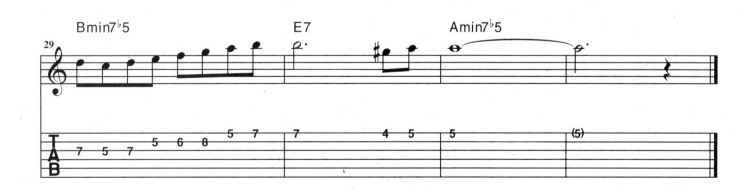